THE CALL
of the
SHEPHERD

Y. M. TIKKUN

Publisher's Cataloging-in-Publication
(Provided by Quality Books, Inc.)

Tikkun, Y. M.
    The call of the shepherd / by Y.M. Tikkun.
    p. cm.
    LCCN 2010933102
    ISBN-13: 978-0-942507-06-5
    ISBN-10: 0-942507-06-1

    1. Meditations.   I. Title.

BV4811.T549 2010   242
                    QBI10-600158

ARTWORK
The front cover art of this book was created by Hadar Krauss,
and is available for purchase as a print at her website: www.hadarfineart.com
Interior and back cover art is by Callie Mitchell.

CAPITALIZATION NOTE
Please note that certain pronouns referring to God in Scripture have been capitalized, even if that is not the case in the original. We have chosen to do this in honor to the Creator. Also, the name satan and related names or titles are not capitalized. We choose not to acknowledge him, even to the point of violating grammatical rules.

Published by Deeper Revelation Books
Revealing "the deep things of God" (1 Cor. 2:10)
P.O. Box 4260
Cleveland, TN, USA 37320-4260
Phone: 423-478-2843
Email: info@deeperrevelationbooks.org
Website: www.deeperrevelationbooks.org

Please visit the publisher's website for distribution information.

${\mathcal{A}}$CKNOWLEDGMENTS

It is written, "The hungry He has filled with good things." This simple scribe has hungered to hear the voice of the Shepherd and to know the desires of His heart for the flock. He has filled my hungry spirit with delicious abundance in speaking these words of *The Call of the Shepherd* into my heart. All glory and all thanks must be given to Him for His generosity and love. The worthiness of the hearer is not a consideration in being given this gift. It is the love of the Shepherd, and His intense desire for His sheep to know Him, which has brought forth this blessing. I bless and honor Him for allowing me to serve as a pen in His gentle hand.

Again, the time of solitude and seeking, necessary to receive this manuscript, would not have been possible, had it not been for the generosity of a godly husband who sent me forth to Jerusalem, while he shouldered the challenges of life and family during my weeks of absence. In addition to Doug's sacrifices, I must acknowledge the selfless gifts of childcare given by our children, Ian and Erin, and by many precious friends, who arose to provide care for Logan, our autistic son.

My dear friend, Pat, set aside the freedom of having all of her children in school, in order to receive Logan as her daytime companion. In spite of the weeks of faithful commitment, she refused any monetary payment for her service of love. May the Lord add richly to her account in Heaven for the hours invested, so that this listener could be free to hear and to write.

Mary, Elizabeth, Laurie, and Diane also gave of their time to help out when Logan needed care. Many other family members and friends supported our family and this work in prayer, giving encouragement, and even delivering meals during my time away to write. The flock gathered around us, and therefore must share in the fruit of this book.

The little apartment which served as my secret garden to meet with the Shepherd was entrusted to me by Anita. The many hours, spent within those walls behind door #7, allowed me to attend to His voice day or night without distraction. Thank you, Anita.

Hadar, my friend and gifted artist, thank you for stretching out in the Spirit to bring forth the cover of this book. May your gifting increase and may the opportunities for you to pour out your calling upon paper and canvas enlarge, bringing even greater blessing.

The person who created the delightful sketches in the interior of this book is someone very close to my heart. Callie Mitchell is my daughter through her marriage to my son. At a time when she was abundantly pregnant with her first child, and then later as a brand new mother, she endeavored, amid the challenges, to produce these excellent drawings, which so beautifully illustrate each chapter. Thank you, precious Callie, for sacrificially contributing to this publication!

Finally, I offer my gratitude to Mike Shreve and Deeper Revelation Books for recognizing the commission for me to write the Shepherd books, and for being used of God to place them into the hands of readers around the world.

$\mathcal{T}$ABLE OF $\mathcal{C}$ONTENTS

FOREWORD

After hearing the *Whispers of the Shepherd* in Jerusalem, my heart was filled with the joy of deep affirmation. I am loved, and I am guided by a gentle and wise Shepherd. To live within His flock is a profound privilege that sets me free to know who I truly am, while at the same time bringing me to the awareness that I have some responsibility accompanying that freedom.

What responsibility does a lamb have to the Shepherd or to the flock? The answer: Once a lamb hears the voice of the Shepherd, the lamb is to follow that voice and obey it. Obedience to His voice not only brings joy and safety, but it brings new growth and maturity. Without applying what we hear and then walking in it, we never truly stretch out and grow. We never prove that His word is true and faithful. If we hear the whispers and simply enjoy the good feeling of being embraced and loved, but never live according to the instruction of His words, we remain immature. What benefit is there of hearing wisdom, but ignoring its call on our lives? Sadly, that is what often happens to lambs in the flock. The things of the world distract them. The pride of the flesh seduces them. The rebellion of the heart rejects the authority of His call, choosing the way of self-determination and experimentation, over His loving call to obey His wisdom. Not only the individual lamb suffers, but the entire flock suffers as well.

All the while, the Shepherd watches, calls, and waits. If His voice is ignored too long, the Shepherd may have to allow the lamb to experience the consequences of willfulness, rebellion, complacency, and pride. Knowing full well that pain and loss will occur, the Shepherd stands by, ready to heal and to embrace, when the sound of the lamb's distressed cry arises out of the resulting brokenness.

We, His lambs, must listen for His voice. *The Call of the Shepherd* is being spoken over the flock in simple parables. It arises as an admonition to come into the life of holiness, humility, submission, and obedience, just as surely as the first book in the series, *Whispers of the Shepherd,* spoke of arising to the embrace of love. Little lambs were designed to grow into mature sheep. With that growth is to come a deeper knowledge and a richer understanding of the Shepherd and of Kingdom realities. Intimacy with the Shepherd increases. Trust in the call of the Shepherd increases to the point that the maturing sheep will follow His voice and obey His instruction regardless of where they lead. Being *with* Him is both the desire and the goal of a mature sheep.

Again, Jerusalem has been the abiding place for this scribe to hear His Call recorded on these pages. However, that is not to suggest that in order to hear and to follow the Shepherd it is necessary to sojourn in Jerusalem, nor does it mean that few people have the privilege of hearing His call. In His own words, He said, *"My sheep hear My voice and they follow Me."* ALL of His sheep can hear His call if they long to hear it … if they long to follow Him. It is His responsibility to speak and to cause us to hear His voice, but it is our responsibility to listen and then to arise to follow. May all the precious members of the flock turn to hear the *call* spoken from His heart to His lambs, and arise to respond.

The Call Of The Shepherd
is for his sheep to mature
in holinesss, humility, and truth.

"I said, 'Age should speak,
and multitude of years should teach wisdom.'
But there is a spirit in man,
and the breath of the Almighty
gives him understanding."
Job 32:7-8

Who may ascend into the hill of the Lord?
And who may stand in His holy place?
He who has clean hands and a pure heart,
who has not lifted up his soul to falsehood
and has not sworn deceitfully.
He shall receive a blessing from the Lord
and righteousness from the God of his salvation.
Psalm 24:3-5 (NASB)

WHO AM I

There are two questions that seem to consume the human mind, little one: #1 Who am I? and #2 Why am I here? When a baby is born, she peers into the eyes of her parents to learn of her value. Is she a cherished daughter or is she a burden? The eyes will convey the message and the embrace or lack of embrace will confirm it to the child. Upon these things the identity of the child will begin to form. As the child grows she may learn of her capabilities and strengths. From these things she may wrongfully conclude her purpose in life. There is more to her purpose upon the earth than what can be found in her abilities and accomplishments.

If the child is ridiculed and told that she can do nothing worthwhile, she is likely to have no sense of why she exists upon the earth at all. Sadly, human parents often fail to bring the important truths to their children because too often they wrestle with their own identity and purpose. They cannot give what they do not have themselves. These unknowing people spend years of their lives trying to discover the answers for their own lives, while often serving as obstacles to anyone else who might be approaching success in finding answers for themselves. This is a perpetuated tragedy based upon a lack of knowledge of who I am. Little one, you were never meant to know or to establish your identity and purpose apart from knowing Me.

It is a priority for Me that you would come to know Me personally. Is it not right for the sheep to become closely familiar with their Shepherd? How can a lamb ever come to trust his life and safety to an unknown authority? Perhaps that is why My flock is so small in these days. The vast majority of the sheep have chosen to live apart from the Shepherd and therefore have no knowledge and no trust of Him. When the wolf or the lion come to attack the flock, the confidence of the sheep will arise only out of their intimacy with their loving Shepherd. They know that He would lay down His life to spare them from death. Those sheep, who choose to live without the Shepherd, open themselves up to destruction as they follow their own heart or as they listen to voices other than that of their wise and loving Protector.

It is time that many more of my human creation would come to know Me. It is time for you, My individually named little one, to know Me on a deeper level. The full vastness of My reality, you could never embrace. The human being is too frail a creature to approach an understanding of My entirety. Know this: there is much more to Me than mere humans or angels can fathom. You can know only that portion of Myself, which I am safely able to reveal to you.

I tell you this about Myself: In Me there is no shadow or dark side. Those who suggest such things are in error. They create an image of Me to match their human mind-sets established out of what they conclude in history. I am perfect love, perfect light, and perfect truth. My ways are often misreported and misinterpreted to cast a shadow on the representation of who I am, but these things are never My reality.

I am not to be measured or contained. I am only known in the measure which I can safely reveal to you. Satan came forth out of the prideful illusion that what the archangel knew of Me was My entirety. He was deluded, believing that what I am was fully known to him, as well as being attainable and transferable to himself. His pride became the blindness leading to his erroneous assumptions, bringing forth his downfall. Even in your lifetime there are those who operate in similar pride, blindness, and assumption about My reality. These created mortals denounce My existence while boldly declaring themselves to be God. All who proclaim their own divinity are walking in the same delusion which is still being propagated by the one who made the first error. It is My will that I should be made known to all people. And yet, unless human beings would become God, knowing My full reality would never be possible. Once the revelation of My reality came to the earth in human form, that revelation was sufficient.

Know also this: No mere human being has full knowledge of My ways and of My plans. I am a keeper of secrets and of much detail until the fullness of time arrives. So why do My human children strive so hard to know all things? It becomes to them an insatiable quest. Why seek to claim the impossible? Yes, all things are possible to Me, but to Me alone are some things possible. Is the fruit of the tree of knowledge of good and evil stuck in your belly? It would seem to be held in place by unholy focus. Yield this piece to Me, and I shall yield My peace to you. All that you need to know I will show you. All the information that you need to have, I will give to you as you need it. Have I not promised you these things? Have I not been faithful? It is enough to know the season while knowing My love for you. Everything will be revealed in its proper time, when you are able to understand and to act accordingly.

My Spirit is vast in His expressions. He will come and instruct you in all matters which I lay before you. He will lead you in a path of truth, wisdom, understanding, wholeness, and safety. Abide in the peace of this truth. Share it with others who have become anxious about their lives.

I am One – but such a One, you can never truly grasp in My entirety. The unity of My oneness is a mystery of which you can only catch a tiny glimmer of understanding. In your current state of being, to see Me face to face, in the deepest, all encompassing sense of My full reality, you could not live. Be content to know Me through the revelation that I have given to you. Read My Word and see. Stretch out in your spirit and touch Me. Receive and rejoice in whatever revelation I allow you to have, while patiently awaiting more, as you are able to contain it. I do not want you to become arrogant by giving you revelation more than you can humbly receive. I do not want you to fall into error, by giving to you more revelation of Myself than you are able to understand. I do not want you to be consumed and destroyed by My reality given in too great a measure for you to contain while abiding in flesh. Trust Me to be who I am, and to reveal that truth to you according to My wisdom. Know that an eternity in My presence will not reveal to you all that I am. It could never be.

For this time of questioning, be content with knowing that I gaze upon you with great tenderness and love. In the reflection of My eyes you will find both your identity and your worth.

You are a dream of My heart, beloved, made manifest upon the earth for joy and for My Kingdom's prosperity. In these things find your purpose. In these realities of Myself find the answers for your reality. I am your Shepherd, little lamb. You are preciously Mine, and I am delighted in you. That is who we are together.

DARKNESS AND LIGHT

In the past I have spoken to you many times about the necessity of staying within My ordained order for creation. However, there is a mixture of human arrogance and human rebellion in your fallen nature that causes you to have great difficulty keeping within My declared boundaries. I put up a safety fence, and you set up competition to see who can jump over it without touching it. I give you a definition and you are inclined to rewrite it to your own need. I declare a law and you try to bend it to accommodate the desires of your flesh.

Do you not understand that your obedience to My order is more than mere safety for you? It is the way for both blessing and wholeness. The order I have created for you is to keep you from confusion, and also to speak to you of My wisdom. In making alterations you not only endanger yourselves, but you miss having the understanding and wisdom that would confirm to you who I am.

Consider the simple thing of determining the beginning of a new day. My Word says that the first day began at evening. Even so, every other day following began at evening. Have you noticed that you consider sunrise the beginning of a new day? Your clock has been ordered by your calculations to begin a new day at midnight. Does My Word suggest that is correct? No. It clearly says the evening was the beginning of the day. As one day ends at sundown, another day begins. Those who revere and honor My Word, continue to hold to My order, thus beginning their new day at sundown as well.

Why is this small detail so important? Is it important to leave My Word intact as I have given it? Or do you believe that it is My Word at all? Perhaps you surmise that what is written is simply an order devised in the minds of men. What have you lost by changing the simple detail of beginning a new day?

In the beginning there was darkness. I chose to begin creation in a state of darkness and then bring forth light. This truth is to express to you that I create wonders out of times in your life which are void of light. I am actively creating even in the dark of night, and in the darkest hours of your life. I am there in the midst of the darkness, hovering over it, breathing upon it and calling the light to come forth. Your day has already begun before you see the light of the morning. Behold, I am there working, creating even before the light breaks upon you. That truth is intended to be a comfort and an encouragement to your heart.

It is written that I ordered light and darkness and separated the day into portions of each. I ordained the night hours of darkness in your day to be a time to sleep – to renew and be refreshed. The labors of the day will be more effectively accomplished after a time of rest. Therefore, I begin your day with rest first, so that the remainder of your day will be lived in strength. I want your day to begin with laying aside the stresses and demands of the daytime; with you coming first to My hand for rest. Why would I want your day to begin with busyness and labor? Without coming first to Me for refreshment, without entrusting your concerns into My keeping before you proceed in your labors … you would be less able to live in wholeness and in joy.

Consider yet another reason why My day for you begins at evening. Do you remember that the Light of the World was born as the stars were coming out? Why was this so? At the beginning of a new day, salvation was born upon the earth. It did not come in the morning sunrise. It did not come at midday in the heat of that hour. Salvation came forth at the beginning of a new day as a declaration to the dark world that the means to defeat its power had come. A new day indeed had begun. Literally, the Light of salvation came serving notice to the darkness that death's defeat had arrived, encroaching on its claimed territory, and defying its power to rule.

In the fullness of time, death was utterly defeated when a grave could not hold in confinement the power of all life. This too happened when it was dark. Only the evidence of the victory was seen in the morning light. The timing of this event is to speak to you of the difficult days coming at the end of the age. At a time when it appears that evil has prevailed and that death has swallowed up the victory of My children, there again shall be a new day emerge out of darkness. At a time when the world languishes in the grasp of wickedness, the light shall burst upon the darkness declaring that the reign of that darkness has ended. This it to remind you of the truth that whenever darkness surrounds you, a new day is already in progress.

Do not wait for the sunrise to lift up songs of praise and blessing. Rejoice in the presence of surrounding darkness for the new day is upon you in the midst of it.

Return to the order I have established for you, little one. Whatever contradictions you have established against My order, now put them aside. I am constantly speaking to you, but you miss the fullness of the messages if you alter them in any way. Listen to My provision and to My blessing being spoken to you through My divine order. Listen to the parables I have placed within every detail of My created order. They are rich and life giving. They bring understanding out of confusion. They bring health out of sickness. They bring peace out of chaos and suffering. Listen. Learn. Live in fullness.

SEASONS

Little one, have you taken note of the order that I have ordained for the world? Each part of the order supports and prepares for another part. Each one speaks a truth that I want you to know. Consider the four seasons of life in each year as they are experienced in your location upon the earth.

There is spring, a season of sprouting and new growth. It brings newness and freshness to the earth. What was asleep in the earth now awakens to begin its progression toward bearing fruit. In this season there may be some harvest brought forth from seed that has continued to grow in the depth of winter. The spring rains come to wash and to cleanse as well as to feed the earth and My children dwelling upon it.

Spring is followed by summer, a time for maturing of the fruit and the beginning of early harvest. There is more heat in the summer, as heat is often the substance of refinement. The sugars in the fruit become sweeter. Summer days are filled with sunlight and less rain. It is a time to care for the maturing fruit and to rejoice in the expectation of the harvest yet to come.

Autumn arrives, bringing many changes. The harvest is now ready. It is begging to be gathered in before its life is exhausted by hanging too long on the branches or vines. The trees prepare for a time of rest in the next season. They yield up their leaves and they return their sap to their roots to sustain them in the days ahead. The rains come again to give the earth a blessing of renewal and refreshment before the days become shortened and cold.

Finally, winter appears. Cold covers portions of the earth. At first there seems to be a battle of wills – shall the day be warm or cold, shall it have sunshine or cloud cover? When the cold settles in and darkness fills more of the day, there is a precious beautification and nourishment that falls from the sky. Snow, whether its arrival is in a flutter or a fury, covers everything with whiteness. When the sunlight breaks through there is a pristine sparkle to the undisturbed snow as it covers the scenery. Leafless trees stand in robes of twinkling white. Birds and animals making their journey across the ground leave tracks behind them in the snow. There is no planting and there is no harvest. This is a time when life goes down deep, to be acknowledged and celebrated in an interior way.

Do you see the parables buried in the seasonal changes that I have written into your life? You cannot change the seasons and their progression even if you would change the order of their names. You could give winter the name summer and it would still be a season of deep cold and falling snow. You could give autumn the name spring, and it would still be the season of taking in the final harvest. But is there more truth to be learned?

I have ordained the same progression of the seasons for each person's life, and yet those dwelling on different hemispheres will have a different experience of season in the same calendar month. The progression remains intact, even though the months assigned to your seasons may not match another's. Perhaps the months, in which you experience the coldness of your winter, will be for another person her months of intense summer heat. Know this: the seasons of human life will proceed even if their position on the tilting earth is different from yours.

The progression is My choice.

Wherever you are located, I will lead you through the same progression from seed through maturity to ingathering and into rest. Even those of My children who abide in the tropical zones or upon the ends of the globe will have seasons to their life experience, even if their climate and surroundings for the most part appear to remain the same. The experiences of each person within their seasons of life are tailor-made. Each experience is intended to bring you into intimate relationship with and understanding of Me.

I want you to know that in your life you will have seasons that are arranged according to My prosperity and according to My plan for your growth. There is joy and fullness contained within each one.

The springtime of your life is to be a great time of awakening; to see things that you have never perceived before. This new understanding becomes a seed planted into the depths of your being, to be watered by the living water I bring. This season is to be a time of patience, awaiting the evidence of new things to be seen in your life from the seeds. Soak in the rains of spring.

Splash and play in them, being washed and renewed before the heat of summer comes.

Summer brings the heat to be applied to the new growth, causing these things to grow even more. This is the time when the fruit, which emerged as a flower, will grow from a small thing to become valuable in its maturity. Its usefulness and bounty is not only to feed you, but many others as well. Use the summer days of your life … attend to the weeds that would rob your plantings of life and health. Pull out anything that threatens your wholeness in Me. Do not scorn the heat that brings forth the sweetness within you, even if it seems to scorch your flesh. Do not long for another season. Enjoy the brightness of this one.

When autumn surrounds your life, do not sit back to take your rest. Arise and harvest. Bring the abundance into the barns to be shared with others and to feed yourself in the days when little grows. Rejoice in the harvest. Rejoice in the changes of color that surround you. Rejoice in the falling leaves that will renew and insulate the ground against the harshness of winter. See the little animals gathering in their stores to maintain them in the winter. They are a sign to you. Some animals will sleep through the winter months ahead and therefore use this season to hoard as much food as possible to sustain them through the time of slumber. You are not to be one of these. Do not take in the abundance for yourself and then sleep while others are awake and in great need. Autumn is not to be a time of self-indulgence in My bounty, but rather a celebration of it, an accounting of it, and a time of storage for future nourishment for you and for others.

Do not cry out against the long, cold days of winter. Instead see the snow beautifying your world, calling you to a greater depth of understanding. Draw down deeply to receive what I bring to you in this time when there are fewer moments of freedom in movement and less fruit to gather. In this season I am preparing you for the glory of the days yet to come. Receive the rest and do not fill these days with frantic plans for the coming days. Come … withdraw into the deep places with Me. Stay with Me; allow Me to be that warm blanket of cover surrounding you, until I call you to come forth out into the world of unique beauty that I have created while you were snuggled in My arms. Use the longer nights to absorb the deep rest they offer you. These winter days are precious and so very important.

Little one, I long for you to delight in My order for you. I long for you to be blessed in each season. Do not long for days that are not yet upon you, nor grieve over the ones past. Live in the current season. Accomplish in this season what I call you to accomplish. Attend to the tasks of the current season with all the focus, strength, and faithfulness that I offer to you. Know that I am good and that My way is good for you. When all the seasons of your life come to their conclusion – when the winter of your life on earth has no spring to follow it, know this: I have a glorious season of newness and delight of which you cannot even imagine. Allow Me to take you gently into this season as you surrender all your seasons upon the earth. The work will be accomplished in you just as I had planned it. The bounty that was grown within you will be seen in My Kingdom, even if others did not see it upon the earth. Come … for now, be content to live in the seasons of your current place of abiding. Each season is taking you a step closer to your place of eternal habitation with Me.

AFRAID TO RELEASE

There are times in your life, little one, when the things you have held on to must be released in order to grasp the new, wonderful things that are being presented to you in the current moment. At times, this will be an exciting and eager release, if you have grown tired of what is in your hand, or if you have found that handhold to now be insufficient for your current need. For example: if you hold in your hand a notebook and pen when someone holds out a laptop computer as a gift for you, you will very easily lay aside the former things that filled your hands, in order to receive the new, wondrous thing. There are times in your life when you are ready to make changes. There will be things offered to you that you can easily see, understand, and find immediate delight in receiving. Whatever has occupied your hands and activities up to that moment, will be easily released and left behind.

At other times, releasing what you have valued and found useful will be difficult. There may be occasions when even the very thought of letting go will fill you with fear. There are two areas of necessary release which many of you struggle against much of the time. These are the things I want you to consider with Me now.

First, I want you to consider the things to which you have grown very attached; finding some form of meaning, security, or purpose for your life by holding on to them. Second, I want you to consider the things that you cling to without even realizing it – things that in reality may be past their season of usefulness and which now have become destructive in their deterioration; or functional things that are working destruction in your life without you even knowing it. In both cases these things may be considered habitual, ingrained, or assimilated into the daily operation of your soul.

Sit with Me for a while to consider the things that you knowingly hold as sources of meaning, security, or purpose for your life, but which are things not necessarily of Me nor called to be part of your journey. These things can be in the form of beliefs, attitudes, opinions, roles, and positions. Even material things and people can be included in this form of cling or release challenge.

There was a time upon the earth, when the authorities of human wisdom and knowledge firmly believed that the earth was a flat structure rather than a sphere. Anyone suggesting that it was round was considered an idiot or a heretic against the powers of the day. Over time the revelation of the world being a globe increased, requiring a test of the theory. Once the test was complete and the reality was clearly established, the images and conclusions of a flat world were released as total ignorance. Before the test was completed and confirmed, the idea of a flat earth was difficult to surrender. Once proven to be false, it was eagerly tossed away.

What are some beliefs that you have held, but which through testing by My Spirit and through experience beyond your expectation, have been proven false? Did at one time, the color of a person's skin speak to you a message about the value and intelligence of that person? This ignorance needed to be struck down and replaced with My truth. Were you at all resistant to releasing it? Did acknowledging that every person of varying skin color from yours is a person of equal value in My eyes cause you to lose any status or value? If you struggled to let go of the delusion, was it due to the fear of losing some of your value to bestow it to another person? Was your personal security threatened by expanding your world to include those you might have held away at arm's length? When you hold a perspective or opinion concerning another person, notice how it affects your own self-evaluation or position. You may find fear, pride, and self-protection playing a role in maintaining a belief when surrounding evidence provided by Me is working to contradict it. Release what does not agree with My evaluation and determination.

Consider the question of material things. Have you ever personally held the belief that people possessing an abundance of material wealth are to receive more honor and esteem than those with less provision? How do you arrive at such a conclusion and formulate that belief? Do you look upon your own wealth and use it as a scale on which you can measure the honor due *you* from others? Does the possession of material wealth give you a sense of security against the threats and surrounding rumors of economic vulnerability? Does your wealth give you the sense of being buffered against the fear of lack? Does abundance in material possession confirm to your soul that My favor rests upon a specific life, even if the person of abundance that you admire gives Me no mention, no thanks, and no honor for the blessings possessed?

Be careful, little one. Material provision is My promise to meet the *needs* of your life, not the *wants* you demand. I provide to both the good and the evil the rain and the sunshine, because I am Mercy. Yes, I do pour out material blessing upon those who I can trust with wealth. However, I may actually hold a greater level of trust and honor for those to whom I have given very little materially. Having very few material possessions does not indicate that I see someone holding a low level of worthiness. It is not to suggest that I cannot trust the one of meager possessions. In their constant love and abiding faithfulness, being content with very little, these children of Mine speak a precious message which the majority of the world needs to hear.

If you have the mind-set of a person's value being indicated by a certain level of material possession, position of power, or physical endowment, release this error in order to receive the truth. Remember that My enemy has gifts to give as well. Very often the unwise have mistaken the abundance provided by the evil one as a sign of My blessings. They do not consider the source or the application of this abundance in the lives of others in the formulation of their conclusions. Release your assumptions to receive My truth. Release the fear of being in poverty concerning material supply. Release and destroy the lenses and scales which you use to evaluate and to measure the hearts of others according to what they have or lack in material supply. Such determinations are Mine alone to make.

Consider your view concerning success and failure, little one. In your understanding you have established a framework by which you measure your level of failure and success, as well as these same evaluations for the lives of others. Beyond the material things we have just considered, what about the applause arising from the hands of the crowd? Do you evaluate a successful person by the amount of applause and regard given to him by other people? When acclaim and acknowledgement from others is missing in your life, do you see yourself as a failure? If a promotion has come to you from a person employing you, is that an absolute indication of your success? What if an unscrupulous manager is rewarding you for operating in the immorality that is familiar and approved by him? Would I applaud your "success"?

Do you hang your certificate of value upon the nail of success as it is framed by the esteem others may declare for you? If the sound of human approval is your measure of success you may advance in the world, while being disqualified in My Kingdom. Remember: if the world loves the way you live and values you for it, most likely you are living outside of My approval. Let go of your need to be applauded and affirmed as valuable by the standards of human beings. Let My approval be your standard and your verification. Do not be afraid of being disapproved by those who do not know Me, or by those who reject My standard of success. Those who receive My applause are people of great love, holiness, submission, mercy, truth, faithfulness, humility, and self control. Certificates of success are given by Me to the overcomers against temptation, and to servants who give of themselves unselfishly without seeking personal gain or acclaim from others.

Now consider with me the things that may have held a place of value in a previous season of your life, but are now misplaced and have become a setup for destruction.

When you were a child, much of the world did not make sense to you. Often you would imagine or pretend a form of reality that brought you comfort and relief. Now in adulthood, it would be unwise to withdraw from a confusing situation in order to construct a mental, false reality … a fantasy out of which you would live and operate comfortably.

When you were a child and something frightened you, you would hide under your bed or under your blankets. As an adult operating in the same way, you would constantly run away from challenges and from things unknown or unfamiliar. You might give yourself permission to remain safely within your own little space in the world, never venturing out to engage in the real joys of life that often are derived through facing a threat or engaging in a refining struggle.

If, when you were a child, you had been demeaned continually by an adult, you might have developed an inner rage prompting you to prove your worth – forming a vow to be more than anyone else had ever been. During adulthood, living out of that rage or out of that vow could fill your life with incessant striving, competition, ill health, and conflict with others. Your life would be filled with stress while lacking trust and true intimacy with those I have intended to be your friends. You would live your life looking for weaknesses in others while formulating ways to prove yourself to be better and stronger. Loneliness and pride would be your constant companions.

If you developed a pattern of avoiding accountability and responsibility in your youth, very likely you would grow into an adult who freely blames and makes excuses for lack and failure. If you also developed the habit of telling lies to cover your sin and to avoid consequences, you might now be a person who has great difficulty in either recognizing or in speaking the truth. In your inner being you may feel like a failure while at the same time working hard at staying in an immature place of irresponsibility.

These are but a few of the patterns and supports that were used by you in childhood. They may have given you a sense of order, safety, value, or freedom in childhood, but now, in this season of your life, they are far from valuable or virtuous. Even though you may find some temporary personal benefit in clinging to them or in applying them, they are still the substance of childish immaturity. They are still taking you down a path toward destruction. Are you afraid to release these habits and patterns? Are you even aware that they exist and operate in your lives? You must release these hazardous, weak ways of thinking and behaving so you can receive wholeness.

You were created to be a high flyer in the Spirit, little one. To live in this manner you must be as a skilled and disciplined trapeze artist. You must be able to move from one challenge to the next … from one opportunity to the next. You must be able to recognize when it is vital to hold on to something secure; but equally vital to realize when to release it to take hold of the next secure thing that I send to you. You must learn to hear My voice and to obey it explicitly, so that you will know the moment of required release. You must know what is safe to grasp and what is not safely tied to a sound and life-sustaining grounding. Childish things must be released and maturity must be allowed to grow. Fear will try to keep you clinging tightly to the things you must release. Fear must be replaced by faith. Insecurity must be replaced by knowing the truth in My secure reality.

If you say that you want to fly through life in victory and joy, surrounded by purpose, you must be willing to take the leap into the life I have ordained for you. Know that as you leap, I will sustain you. I will catch you in your weakness. I will train you and I will applaud you. When I call for you to grab on to what I send, grab on firmly with My strength. When I say to release, let go, even if the new thing coming to fill your hands is not yet in view. Never let fear delay or eliminate your obedience, causing you to come to a standstill, causing your hands to fail, causing you to fall. Stretch out in confidence! Grab hold in a spirit of true commitment. I am your success and I am your ability.

Release ... take hold ... fly!

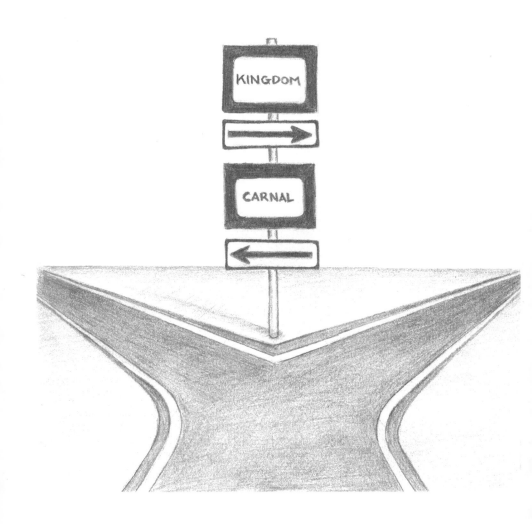

DECISION MAKING

How do you arrive at a decision, little one? Do you consider your course in solitude or do you seek the counsel of others? What source of wisdom do you consult? Is there a format you choose to follow in the belief that it will lead you to a good decision?

Too many decisions are being made by My children without consulting Me. There was a time and there was a place in days past, when I was the center point of all decisions made concerning the people of Israel. The prophets sought My wisdom and My approval when there was a decision to be made on behalf of the nation. My word was then relayed to the kings and to the authorities. Who is consulted now? The ones who make decisions now fling words and thoughts of their own perspective into the atmosphere as they try to outdo each other in knowledge and in reasoning as they volley for power and authority. Are their thoughts and words merely the tools of wisdom, or are they actually wisdom in themselves?

Look at the fruit of these dialogues and monologues to find the answer to this question. Notice that these people are ever speaking while seldom truly listening. They are ever hearing without understanding. They are ever seeing with fractured and filtered lenses. They think they possess wisdom; they believe they are filled with understanding.

These who govern the nations of the world are filled with error. It is even so with those who govern as shepherds over My flock. So few truly seek My face for the truth. Too many come only seeking validation for themselves and for their perspectives. Those who seek Me at all often come to find confirmation and support for the course they have already determined on their own and have committed to follow. If they share the need for a decision with others, it is often done so among their supporters – among those of like mind who will rarely challenge a decision that has been formulated. They confidently decide without ever truly considering My will, My way, or My Word. It was done this way in the days of old. It continues to be the same in these days of comfortable prosperity.

Each of you is part of some form of government. In some areas of governance you lead, and in others you only follow. In addition to being under the governmental authority of human leaders, you are to be operating within My Kingdom's government. Yet, of those who lead, who governs out of the Spirit of the Holy One? Most leaders govern out of human soul. Many govern out of an unholy spirit rather than out of Mine. The flock lives in a poverty that has not come to them out of My decision, but out of a choice to live in a self-made kingdom rather than in Mine.

Where are My chosen few – those Kingdom dwellers who are called to lead, that I might lift them up as an example to others? Little one, are you prepared to be lifted up as an example for others to follow? Do you, My chosen, fear being different and being obvious in comparison to the rest of the world's inhabitants? Do you tremble at the thought of being at cross purposes with the world powers and personalities? Where is the holiness that My Word requires?

Compromise is the way that many of you choose. Murmuring and manipulation have become your manner. Whenever those, who are given the charge of making decisions, gather to confer, they vie for position and for power. Rather than seeking after truth from a spirit of humility, their own pride drives their conclusions. The world has become a playground infested with bragging bullies, and often My little ones join the gang. Is this the way you are to be found operating within my own flock?

If truth is light and the world is covered in darkness, where are those called to shine brightly in that darkness? Have the selected leaders developed such a tender fellowship with darkness that the light is too painful to tolerate? Do they place lenses upon their eyes to modulate the light, and to protect their eyes from its glare? I see it is so.

In the examining light of a physician's lamp, the scabs and sores are seen upon the body. The warts and the tumors, the brokenness and the disease become evident in the presence of its illuminating power. The power of a deeper light of revelation is applied for hidden disease, creating revealing images for the physician to see. Who would want to behold such ugly, damaged things? Only one, who may wish to be healed and directed toward the paths of health, would eagerly seek the light and the examination. Only one, who would desire to reveal hidden things to bring them into the truth of understanding and wholesome solutions, would apply the deep light. Is it possible that those who lead others would prefer to walk in the darkness – in the power of delusion – rather than to be subjected to the painful reality that healing is needed within them as well?

Only one who understands that to be human is to be fragile and vulnerable without the truth would seek after such examination continually. Only one who understands that self-diagnosis often leads to error would be willing to seek the evaluation of a higher source of truth. Decisions concerning wholeness and direction must be made out of truth, not out of human evaluation. Decisions made which are based on a false evaluation of wholeness contain inevitable weakness and destruction.

Consider this question, little one: is the course, now being set by decisions, contrived through human reasoning so secure that one would not want to be turned from it by the promptings of genuine truth and by godly wisdom?

I tell you, surely there are decisions being made in the halls of authority that will bring grave consequences if they are made outside of My wisdom. The best plans of men will be as grass before a raging fire. In the wake of the fire there will be much devastation. The reasoning of men is warped and perverted by input from wounded and diseased souls resulting from unholy input from the great deceiver.

It is written, *"lean not upon your own understanding ... "* Why then do men not only lean upon it, but also stand upon it confidently? *"In **all** your ways acknowledge Me, and I shall make straight your path."* I shall do it – I shall direct your path as you consult with Me, and as you seek after My truth in all decisions.

Pray that those who are making decisions without Me will be consumed in their own confusion, rather than leading many into destruction. Pray that they will foresee the outcomes of their decisions before they materialize into reality. My truth is a pillar of clarity, even as human reasoning apart from Me is a swirling cloud of nonsense. Pray that those who seek answers will seek Me first.

There are those in My flock who place themselves in a mind-set that declares that I am not concerned with the details of daily human choices. They boldly announce that My will for them is to use their own brain power to decide the incidentals of their lives. These sheep are not familiar with My heart for them. Little lambs and elder sheep have within them the desire to walk, to eat, and to engage in the choices of their own hearts; perceiving these things to be the best course. The Shepherd not only stands near to watch and to protect, but also to guide them in each step.

I shall lead you in the way of all truth – *all* truth. Know that the truth required for wholeness and wisdom in every decision, no matter how small, comes from Me. Simply seek that truth from My heart for you in every decision. In this way you shall prosper, not only in wholeness, but also in true humility and in deep intimacy with Me. This is My heart for you, little one, and for all of My precious flock. Decide to entrust Me with every decision you are facing, and I shall always give to you My best answer, as I draw you to My heart to perceive it.

DISRUPTION

Little one, have you ever noticed how quickly your soul is given over to anger when being disrupted from your set course? I speak of many disruptions, both small and large. I speak of many incidents that break into your day whether you are in a place of rest or activity, leisure or work, wanderings of the mind or in intense focus. The flow of the mind reacts to being interrupted. The direction of the emotions and the course being followed by the body note the impact of a disruption and respond to it. Sometimes the response is a reactionary irritation followed by a quick return to the course of endeavor or focus.

Why does the disruption capture your attention at all? Does the level of response depend upon the length or upon the intensity of the invasion? Do you respond the same to both an accidental interruption as you do to an intentional disruption? Another consideration for you is this: are you responding only to the nature of the disruption itself, or are you also responding to its source – to the person or thing bringing the disruption? What then is your response?

Why am I asking you to consider these things? It is because I have a plan for your life that was established at the beginning of time. It is a plan that, when followed, will fill your life with meaning, joy, and prosperity. You, with your freedom of personal will, can choose My plan or your own. Beyond yourself and Me, there is another one who would like to influence your life's journey as it is moving toward prosperity in Me. The great usurper, the enemy of your soul, constantly seeks to distract you from your successful journey, if he is not able to remove you from it directly.

One of his greatest tools is disruption through distraction and timely incursions into your focus or timetable. If he is successful, he is able to slow you down and tie you up with unimportant things, making them seem as great mountains or urgent issues. Inspiring you to anger toward another person is a way that he can tie up your emotions and thereby pull you off the course of peace and right thinking. You need to be aware of his intentions and of his methods.

Still there is another reason why you may be experiencing disruptions in your day – Me. I might just be breaking into your inner world or into your calendar to introduce something new to you. I may be using a moment to teach you something vital, as I draw your attention to where I would have you focus for instruction. I might even be intentionally pulling you away from a hazard or from an obstacle right in front of you, but yet unperceived by you. Perhaps I am giving you the honor of turning aside to help, to teach, or to lift up another person who is nearby, allowing you to be My hands, My voice, or My embrace.

It is very important to discern the true source of any disruption. Are you being disrupted by Me, by My enemy, or by human flesh alone. If I have seized a moment from you, whether directly or through another person, rejoice and yield to the disruption. If My enemy has sought to pull you out of your peace and off course, simply turn away and refocus to continue in your previous direction. If undisciplined or immature flesh comes to invade a moment of purpose in your day, extend grace, and in love, teach the way to respect the time of another person. Do not battle and do not waste time in flurries of emotion. Move on and return to your day and to its requirement.

Now turn your attention again to the responses you make when being disrupted. If the disruption has been slight, or perhaps one made by accident, then the response is less severe. More grace is extended to the unintentional disruptor than to the purposeful one. If, however, the disruption is unproductive, intentional, and repetitive, if it is seen as willful and insensitive, then there is a larger and deeper impact, soliciting a more severe response. During such an occasion, do you feel in your heart, the initial uprising of irritation? If the emerging annoyance is not discontinued, or if the disruptor is unrepentant, this irritation soon grows into anger.

A conflict of territory is established in your mind. Whose time is it? Whose space is predominant? Whose work is more vital? Whose course is more holy? Are these not the considerations of the soul? Are these not the questions that burn within your heart and within your reasoning, as the insult of the disruption is considered? Are these considerations not questions of personal entitlement? Who is entitled to the moment, and for what purpose has it been ordained? Stirring up entitlement and territorial conflicts are specialties of My enemy. He presses upon the human "self" in an attempt to create the atmosphere of competition and jealousy based upon assumptions.

In your interactions with people, it is wise to consider these things. There must be a settling and an agreement of understanding, so that conflicts do not abound. There must be a generosity of such things as time, place, and purpose. If you think that your own occupation of a given space and time is more significant and purposeful than that of another, then you will be markedly vulnerable to anger in disruption. You will find yourself being deprived unjustly of that which is rightly yours – that being your peace. Your mind will be filled with assumptions and with accusations about the one disrupting. Has the disruption been hostile and full of intent? Has it been calculated to send a message of disdain? Does the disruption come to rob you of that which is rightfully yours?

These considerations apply not only to an invasion of your space and your time, which alter or stall your course of movement, they also apply to disruptions breaking in upon your beliefs and upon your understanding. If what you hold in your set of beliefs is actual truth, then surely truth will not be moved, even if it is bumped by an opposing view. Why would you fear the invasion of a suggestion that a portion of your beliefs should be removed or changed? Truth will always stand. The disruptive assertions will fall away, being ineffective to bring a change in your values and foundational understanding. Is it an insult that you have been made to pause to consider them? Why? If you are the bearer of truth, would it not be most generous to listen to those who are in need of such truth? Your disruption of time may heal their disruption of truth, so that truth might again flow in another human life.

Is it possible that you sometimes angrily defend that which is not so surely a truth, but only a point of view to which you cling? Is your defense of an idea a way of trying to influence others into confirming your thoughts as truth? Are you hoping that in confirming your point of view as right, that they will be validating <u>you</u>? In your own thinking you can be in error. Do not seek others to validate your error or to validate you. Remember, I am the Author of absolute truth, and I shall not be moved. I need no validation. Stand with My truth and you shall not stand in error. Neither will you ever have to find validation in others, since I am your validation. You are to agree with the truth I bring, not to defend yourself, in bringing it to others. That is a difficult distinction to make and an even more difficult discipline of flesh to accomplish.

Is this issue of dealing with disruptions also a question of generosity? Does it not sift down to the question of possessions?

I have set you upon this earth to be in the company of others. I have done this for both your joy and for Mine. I have provided you with all things. Truly, all things are Mine. Is it not arrogance to think that anything solely belongs to you? If I possess your spirit, as you have given it to Me in rebirth, is anything left to your possession? Yes, and also no. I have given you a free will. You may surrender it to Me, so that it is no longer yours. And yet, you have the freedom to take it back and make it yours again, at any given moment. If I am the Keeper of your will, shall I not also possess your minutes and all of your supply within those minutes? Whatever is Mine – will it ever be truly robbed from you or from Me?

You human children do not deal with each other in the generosity, in the compassion and grace that I would demand. You set your own feet and your own hands; you set your minds and your mouths too often on a course that you have determined for yourself. If someone should intersect with this course, asserting her or his own priority on top of yours, there is an occurrence of hardened offense which can be given life by your sense of insult, if you give it power beyond the present moment. Resentment and unforgiveness abound where there is a lack of generosity.

How would I want you to live together? I want you to look at the choices you have made for the course of your life honestly. I want you to accurately see what you have created for yourself and for your day. Whatever you possess for yourself can be assaulted, and robbed by another person. Confess then these things, which you have held back from Me – all these things which are to have been Mine. I want you to look honestly at the arrogance which is reflected in your actions and in your words with others. Repeatedly you say, in defense of your negative response to disruption that, "My course is greater in worth and significance than yours." To this I would ask you: "Who has held the measuring tool, and by whose eye has the gage been read? Through what lens has the eye seen the measurement"?

Oh, little one, are your self-entitled plans so dear to you, that you would cause others to be frustrated in theirs? Is your course so vital and so sure that you are without repentance for the toes you crush, and for the time you leave unredeemed in others? Could you not consider what is precious in each moment, and then offer that precious thing to each other in love?

Put aside your insults and your anger. Put aside your sense of violation arising from the elements of your day being disrupted by others. Give Me the very course of your life. Be generous enough to allow others to give Me those same things. If they will not yield their course to Me, do not allow their refusal to concern you. This is to be My work and My consideration with them, not yours. If My assignment for you is to deliver a word to another person for his course correction, that word will arise out of Me, not out of your own soul. My words will always convey deep love, even if they are firm and challenging. If My words are mingled with your own soulish concerns and judgments for the other person, they will be invalidated, and could even be harmful. My message of truth could be buried under your layer of human judgment, to be totally lost in translation. In this case, your expression of soul will have become a disruption in the course I am presenting to another one of My children. You see, you must discern what disruptions are occurring within yourself, lest you become a disruption to another.

Truly I say to you, if you turn to Me, and seek My guidance with each perceived disruption, you will find that nothing has been lost. I will identify for you the source of the disruption. If it is unholy, you can simply disregard it to continue on in your day. If you take the time to discover what is of Me in your disruptions, you will find that something has actually been gained. Through My specific disruptions delivered into your day, you will often find that I have inserted gifts for you of pure treasure. For if nothing else, in the act of turning to Me at the moment of My disruption, you shall see My smile. You shall feel the warmth of My heart as you turn away from the coldness of your own heart and the busyness of your day to notice Me. As you receive what I have chosen to bring to you, in the midst of the disruption, you will discover, and will come to understand in your inner being, that *all is on course*.

DREADED TARANTULAS

Little one, consider with Me the things that you dread. What is it that makes your stomach sickened at the thought of having to face or encounter it as you make the journey through your life? What is it that by even the thought of it, your skin manifests a crawling sensation and your heart an inclination for escape? Just the mere thought causes you to want to flee in fear from the suggestion or images formed in your mind. Such a thought, such a possibility creating this kind of response is the substance of dread to your heart.

Many of My children shudder at the thought of meeting a tarantula as its eight furry legs would cross their path. Is it the sight of this creature alone that frightens you, or the thought of it actually touching you in some way? Is it the appearance and movement that sickens your stomach, or the fear of its painful and sometimes deadly bite? These questions are important for you to consider, as their answers provide clues to the power of dread in many areas over your life.

Consider your size and the size of the tarantula. Who is greater? Surely you have the greater dimensions; and yet in the moment that a tarantula bursts into your presence, there is often an instant feeling of vulnerability and weakness.

Which has more speed in making an escape – you or the eight-legged opponent? Although he has six more legs than you have, you have the advantage of greater leg length and the need to coordinate only two rather than eight in order to move away. So often I see your two legs freeze and cease to function when they have all the advantage to move away from a threat to your peace.

There is something about both the appearance and the way in which this creature moves about – the makeup of its physical form – that frightens you. The silence of his approach, the uninvited invasion, stirs your soul to dread; but there is more to your fearful response than these things. His movement occurs most freely at night under the cover of darkness while the darkness of his color conceals him. He maneuvers about quickly in any direction of his choice – a direction which you cannot determine, whether a crawl or a jump. The hairy covering of his body can conceal him from you until suddenly his abrupt movement announces that he is hiding in a corner or near a rock. Your mind tells you that spiders of this size carry a geometrically increased threat proportional to their mass.

This creature prefers the darkness for his operations while you were designed to prefer the light. There is a natural opposition between you and these creatures, but there is more to feed the power of your dread than only this. Anything that moves under the cover of darkness, with the power to impose itself upon you with the potential of causing harm, suggests threat to your heart. Anything that delights in being concealed in the dark places is something to be mistrusted. Any creature that carries venom to be injected into another life through a bite is something to create objection in the human heart. I designed you with inner cautions and with inner revulsions to things that are opposite to the life, to the brightness of My truth and to the honest transparency that is to be the hallmark of My children. But I did not create you with this alarm of dread.

Terrorizing surprise – the advent of something hideous to your soul bursting upon your life causes you to feel vulnerable and often faint hearted. The messages that come with this threatening surprise is that you are alone to face the threat and that you are ill equipped to deal with it. Your mind tells you that you need time to plan for a response, but the sudden onset of a threat takes away your ability to plan your defense. The time to deal with the threat is urgent now. The threat seems to have more power because you have found yourself without the ability to control the movement of the threat. It may pursue you on the run, or it may jump to attach itself to you. Do you feel trapped and helpless at the mere thought of these things? Creating these impressions is the very goal of a spirit of Dread.

Dread seeks to manufacture within your soul the scenario of your vulnerability and impending harm before such a thing is truly a reality. Dread seizes your imagination and writes a script outlining your defeat by a threat which you do not currently face. How many of you have worried over a physical symptom, but delayed seeking the counsel of a physician due to the dread of what the problem might be? Dread has taken a position of power within your mind and body. It has caused you to freeze at the mere thought of an overwhelming threat. Its numerous legs have spoken to your heart and you cannot run fast enough to avoid the reality of the threat overtaking you and biting you.

But what if a threat comes upon you and proves to be real? Who among you has heard the word *cancer* fall from the lips of your physician and immediately succumbed to the dread of your own suffering, loss, and death? Had I announced such things over your life? Did you inquire of Heaven for My determination and plan concerning your well-being? So quickly My little ones are given over to panic and conclusions of defeat in their lives when words or images paint a picture of loss and pain across their minds and hearts. The suddenness of the threat's appearance leaves My children with the feeling that they are vulnerable and unprepared. They cannot tell which way the threat will move. It comes enwrapped in darkness, filled with venom.

Little one, you need to clearly determine what is the true threat and what is the envisioned dread. Do not respond to the dread or you will be less able to deal with the threat. If you believe the images and words of the dread, you will give it the power to make you weak and vulnerable to a level of attack that you do not currently face.

There are tarantulas in the world. Some of you live in their environment on a daily basis. Are you to make friends with them and invite them into your house? No! When they invade your space, you are to eject them immediately. You are to put them under your feet. You are to keep your doors closed and your drains, through which they might enter, closed. Your windows may need to be screened so that you can allow the fresh air to enter your dwelling, while refusing entrance to the invaders. Will you ever get used to the threat of their appearing? Perhaps not, but you will learn that they do not have power over your responses to their presence. Learn to discern their advance against you. Know the times when you are feeling vulnerable and set your face toward a posture of overcoming whatever crosses your path. You have authority over the creatures of the earth. Apply your authority and stand upon it.

When it comes to the tarantulas in your life, other than the eight-legged ones, you need to again know your authority and to stand upon it. You need to know the truth in the midst of real threat and to allow it to speak more loudly than the voice of dread. You must know that you are never alone. When you are unable to prepare for a sudden assault, know that I have already prepared a victory for you against it.

There are true threats in this life that can startle you and bite you. Entrust your encounter with each one into My hands. As you belong to Me, I am your guard and your protection. Nothing will come to harm you that has not been seen in advance by My eyes. I can see all things that lurk in darkness. I see every threat. I have a plan of victory to deal with those real threats.

I also see the illusions that dread spins in the darkness to cause you to faint at the mere thought of threat. Dwell in the light of truth, little one. Never make peace with darkness and deceitful illusions. Do not listen to their suggestions of defeat and death. Do not welcome the tarantulas into your dwelling in order to make a bargain with them. Dread will not be contained by any of your contracts made with it. Renew your mind as you have it washed and secured by My truth. There is enough challenge in your present day reality. You need not add to the possibility of defeat by embracing dread to add to your understanding of the future. Again, you have authority over the lies and illusions of the deceiver. Use it!

The days ahead will have many challenges and many threats. The images now being sent forth against My children of faith are intended to cast dread into their hearts and minds so that they will leave My flock to save themselves from threat. Remember to reject the illusions and embrace the truth. My word is absolute truth. Cling to it. Even in the days of very real threat and loss to My own, there will be victory. Wherever there is pain and loss it will be short and temporary, only creating a doorway to an eternal joy and gain. Do not live in dread of the coming days.

Lift up your foot, little one. Consider the many tarantulas that lurk in your mind and heart. Drive them out and then crush them under your foot. Use your authority to send the truth of it crashing down upon the illusions of death and defeat. I am your complete victory. I am the substance of your life. No threat and no tarantula can overcome you as you abide in Me.

FRYING PANS
AND FIRES

Little one, you have seen that the heat of fire can cause things to burn to destruction. You have also seen that when carefully applied, these same things of heat and fire can prepare delightful food for you to eat. That which would be unsafe or unsavory before cooking, can be changed by these potentially destructive things into something useful, delicious, and pleasing. Something unusable can be made into something valuable by properly applying the qualities of heat and fire.

Not only must you consider the appropriate application of this power, but also the appropriate place to contain the fire and heat. Within a home a fire burning brightly in the hearth can bless the household as it protects the family from the chill and cold of the season surrounding it. The cooking pot can thrive in its service to the family as a contained fire is carefully directed beneath it. But what will happen if the fire is improperly contained, or if it refuses to remain within set boundaries? That same power of heat and fire blessing the house can quickly become a terror and a threat. If it was allowed to move about within the house, uncontained, very quickly the house itself and its residents could be totally destroyed by its power.

Consider the simple frying pan. This cooking tool was created out of a substance designed to tolerate heat and fire – but only to a degree. Beyond a certain point, beyond the boundaries of tolerance to heat established in the nature of its metal, even the frying pan can be destroyed. This is true also for every item placed within the frying pan in preparation for eating. Some ingredients must be heated gently and mildly. Others can tolerate higher temperatures and longer exposures to the heat. It is wise to consider the character, boundaries, and tolerance of each individual item you intend to add to the pan before you expose it to the heat of cooking. Delicate and fragile food can lose desired character and quality very quickly by being added carelessly to high heat. Flavor will be lost. What was delicate can be made brittle or overly soft if the needs of the item are not considered. Hard, heat-resistant, dense, thick food pieces can be subjected to heat in a greater degree and for longer periods of time than the light and thin. Leafy vegetables will perish if treated like raw meat. Raw meat exposed to the frying pan as if it was a cluster of fresh spinach might well leave the pan as inedible.

I call you to wisdom and to understanding in considering these things, little one. I speak not only about the realities of fire, but also about similar realities found in the use or misuse of various forms of power. I am speaking to you of these things for you to consider carefully the boundaries, the character, the application, and the individuality of whatever is exposed to the heat and fire of powerful things.

You have power in your words, little one. You have power in your love. You have power in the expression of your emotions. You have power in the exercise of your authority and position. You must be mindful of this. Furthermore, you must be aware of the nature and condition of others who will be exposed to your fire. You need to understand that having power does not mean that it is wise or safe to apply its fire whenever you are inclined to demonstrate it. Not every place and situation is suitable to contain it. If you use the fire of words, emotions, position, and authority carelessly and beyond the proper boundaries that have been established by Me, you will bring destruction.

You have been entrusted with the ability to bring change in the lives of others. You can bring positive change or destructive change. You can use your counsel and rebuke to tenderize someone to a more useful state, or harden someone to bitterness and rebellion. You can apply the heat of the position I have entrusted to you to enable others to rise to a new level of fruitfulness and opportunity, or you can burn them with the heat of your ego causing them to shrivel and withdraw. Your words of empowered faith can cook fear out of a person who is seized by dread, while your hot words of legalistic doctrine can destroy a fragile faith. I designed you to be creations of power and of fire, but not to be self-directed in either.

Having considered your heat and fire, now consider Mine. There is fire in My Word. There is fire in My love for you. There is fire in My passion for the qualities of My nature to be expressed in your life upon the earth. I place each one of My children upon the frying pan of life, applying the precise amount of heat, for the precise amount of time in order to prepare them for victorious living and for eternal glory. The time in My frying pan, determined by My wisdom, is intended to complete your processing time, enabling you to emerge from the heat as a useful and savory food to nourish a starving world. I alone must apply the heat. I alone must determine its degree, for I alone know the nature, the character, the tolerance, and the perfect outcome for each one of My children. Only I know what the finished product should look like and how it should taste. This comes not only out of My knowledge and out of My great plan, but also deeply out of My great love.

The fire and heat, the surface upon which I choose to process you may not be to your liking; but they are not for you to avoid or to judge. Trust and submit to My application of heat and to My positioning of you in the place to receive it. If you wish to serve Me and My purposes you must trust and submit, rather than design your own way to perfection, fulfillment, and meaning.

Look for a moment to the lives of others who are in the heat of their frying pans. Have you ever applied the powerful heat of your words to accuse, to judge, or to criticize? Have you ever added your fire to Mine to hurry along the processing or to punish someone in your own self-righteous anger? Have you been aware of the destruction, breakdown, or hardness that has come into the hearts of those exposed to your fire? Have you been tempted to discard those who in your judgment have become unsuitable or unpalatable for your tastes? Search your heart. Search your history of relationships and interactions with others.

Have you ever criticized My choices for you or for others? Have you made efforts to turn down the heat within your frying pan or turned it up for someone else? Have you ever made excuses allowing you to exit from the frying pan of your life? Have you ever offered a way of escape for those being "cooked" by My hand? Have you ever added cool water to lower the temperature only to find out later that you widened the path of destruction by creating scorching steam in the midst of fire? Have you ever tried to crawl out of My hot frying pan, believing that is was unjust or totally an attack of the enemy?

You have done all of these things at some time, little one. When you respond to the heat in your life and in the lives of others in these ways, you deny that My hand is the greater authority at work. You accuse My invested attention and My goodness. Yes, at times I will allow the enemy to add fuel to the fire, but I alone direct the duration and intensity of the fire and heat.

It is necessary for Me to apply heat to your life. It is vital that I set you in the places where the heat will be applied. Sometimes you and others are rebellious and hardened by your arrogance and pride. A period of time in My frying pan can soften your heart and flesh to a precious repentance and submission. At times there may be something within you that needs to be purged out – something that is either destructive or which will diminish your usefulness and flavor. There might even be something deadly within you that must be cooked out before the disease of this sin finds its victory in your destruction, or be passed on to sicken others as they dine upon your substance.

There is yet another reason why I place you in the midst of My heat and upon the hot surface of the frying pan. If you are a spiritually healthy, obedient, and submitted child of Mine, I may wish to bring the fire to refine you to a higher perfection. I may choose to bring you through the fire to change you into a higher form for My glory. I may choose to add the fragrance and flavor of a testimony of victory over adversity in your life—a precious gold which is acquired only through exposure to great heat. The fire of My refining touch may be My way to greatly bless you and others through you. Too often the fire of promotion is evaluated by the undiscerning or by the judgmental as a sign of My severe disapproval. How great an error this is!

I want you to deeply consider what I am speaking to you in all this. I have told you that My way is refinement, bringing you to a place of strength and maturity. You are to arise in strength and proceed onward into even greater strength. You are to shine with glory after your time in the fire – shining even more brightly, giving off greater heat and light as time passes. I will choose the way of your journey. I can sovereignly promote or I can refine in fire. I can seat you in the center of a heated frying pan to humble you, or cause you to stand in a high position; being a light to all those around you.

I will do whatever I will do to increase your quality, usefulness, and eternal beauty. Allow Me to do this in your life, trusting in My wisdom and love. Do not mingle the fire of your soulish evaluations, assumptions, and judgments with the work of My hand in your life or in the lives of others. Trust! Submit! Never try to remove yourself from My hot frying pan. Your time of processing is vital. This is the way to wholeness and glory. This is the way to find truth and fulfillment. Do not interfere with the refinement of others by trying to protect them from My heat. The frying pan is the way to reach the perfection that I have ordained for you to have in the midst of a flawed world.

When My plan for your life is complete, I will not take you from the frying pan and drop you into an eternal fire. Never! Rather you shall be gently lifted from the refining fire to a place far beyond all destructive fire. You shall be as polished gold set in a high place of My presence, where the only fire surrounding you will be the blaze of My passionate love and the brilliance of My glory forever.

HEARTS AND POMEGRANATES

Your heart is so very precious to me, little one! It is not only the physical heart that I cherish, but also your heart of soul and spirit. Your physical heart has been made to bring the perpetual flow of lifeblood through your body. Your heart of soul and spirit has been designed to propel a constant flow of life to and from My heart. Both aspects of the human heart are to sustain life – one, a physical life, and the other, a spiritual life. If either heart is blocked or ceases to function, death approaches to take away the vitality of life.

A physical heart, in its deep red color and its steady, strong, and constant beat, speaks of health. If this same heart was to wither or to expand beyond its created design – if it was to become irregular or labored in its beating, the whole body would become weak and sickened. The deep red color of life can quickly be changed to a color of blue. The hue of the body's skin likewise will move to a pallor of gray or blue. This is a sign that urgent repairs of the heart are desperately needed, through the physician's hand or sovereignly through the Shepherd's hand. Such a wounded or sickened heart would need to be carefully opened, probed, and repaired to restore health and renew the flow of life.

The signs of a healthy heart of soul and spirit are important to note as well, little one. One with a healthy heart in this case has a certain brightness of heart color which is evidenced through the eyes. One with a healthy spiritual heart has a light in the eyes. In such a person of a healthy heart abides a life-giving power and a steadiness – a functional beat in words and actions. The color of love is visible in the outward appearance. An invisible strength from this heart passes strength to the human body surrounding it.

If the heart of soul and spirit was to become sick, this too would bring evidence of its deteriorating condition. There arises a labor and a constriction in its love which may be hidden at first, but which cannot be dismissed over time. The eyes darken while the actions and words demonstrate a certain blueness of color. Rather than being a conveyor of life, such a heart in its irregular, measured beating loses power and uses all of its strength to maintain itself. Sometimes the disease of this heart is found to be a slow and progressive hardening. Sometimes it is a violent rupture resulting from an injury, real or perceived. Attending to the disease and dysfunction of this heart is as urgent as the need to attend when there is disease and dysfunction in the physical heart.

Dealing with the disease and dysfunction of the heart, whether physical or soul/spirit in nature, is a vital endeavor. Those who physically open and probe the heart need great wisdom and great training to accomplish their work effectively. Likewise, those who hope to probe and to open the soul/spirit heart must also be trained and skilled. Surely I tell you, it is easier to find a skilled and wise surgeon of physical hearts than it is to find one for the soul/spirit hearts. Hours of study and training combine with many hours of surgical experience to make a heart surgeon from a medical student. Hours of study, mentoring, and practicum are required to bring forth a certified healer of the soul/spiritual heart, but the measurement of the success for this caregiver is far less easy to determine.

Too many people who have the desire to heal soul/spiritual hearts, lack the wisdom, the discernment, the anointing, and the love to hold the heart of another – even if they have the professional credentials to do so. Many caregivers and leaders find themselves faced with diseased and broken soul/spiritual hearts within those who work under their charge or who dwell within their own families. Without taking many steps in any direction upon a road, you will find someone walking around with a diseased soul/spiritual heart. Surrounded with this great need, but unprepared to effectively enact healing, these leaders and caregivers often engage in a careless effort, which brings only more pain. Self-made practitioners of heart surgery are everywhere. They can be found in the secular world or in the religious community. Some have truly good intentions, while others seek to address the pain and dysfunction in the lives of others to avoid the inspection and diagnosis of their own sickened heart. Those who lack the depth of truth in their own lives often try to apply their version of truth into the lives of others. Sadly the diseases of the heart not only continue, but they spread to others in this way.

Know this: I am the healer of all hearts. I have both the love and the wisdom. I have the compassion and the mercy combined with the cutting edge of truth. I have chosen and trained servants among you who are gifted in this endeavor of heart repair. Seek only My servants to hold, to open, and to diagnose the healing of your wounded or diseased heart.

You will know them not only by their fruit, but you will know them by the reflection of My life presence in their eyes. These servants will not profess to have knowledge and skill of their own making, even if they are educated in an academic field of healing. They will not require of you a high material price to bring My healing into your life. They will not take the glory and honor from a successful "operation" but will give those things back to Me. Most importantly, My servants will not take your heart in their hands to rip it open for exposure, as others do. They leave the method of heart exposure to Me – following My individual instruction specific to each wounded person.

Consider with me the beautiful pomegranate, little one. Pomegranates represent the hearts of My children to Me. This precious fruit has the beautiful red color of life on its exterior. It often is nearly the size and shape of the human heart, although with much more fullness. At its top is a small crown to indicate My desired Lordship over each heart.

The contents of the pomegranate's heart are very precious. Often the untrained surgeon of the pomegranate's interior will cut it deeply to rip open the fruit, tearing at its support membranes and tissues to retrieve the luscious little packets of red juice and seeds. Those who operate in this way dig away at the heart causing their fingers to be severely stained and juice buds to fly everywhere. A pile of discarded support tissues are on the floor or all around the waste bin. It is a messy and destructive process. Ah, but there is a better way to find the treasure within the pomegranate!

Someone with love for this fruit and with a passion to obtain its treasure buried within will be willing to labor to accomplish the task in a more careful way. A large bowl of water will be filled. A gentle cut will be made tenderly through the hard skin.

The pomegranate will then be totally immersed in the water, as careful hands open it up while fully submerged. The fingers will tug and rub at the support membranes which have held the juice and seed packets in place. This operation will continue until all the beautiful little red packets have been released from their hiding places. The treasure of the undamaged little packets will sink to the bottom of the basin. The unnecessary debris of the support fibers will float to the top to be skimmed off and discarded. The hands of the pomegranate surgeon will emerge from the water unstained, filled with an abundance of treasure to be enjoyed and shared.

How does this apply to the extraction of treasure from human hearts? There is treasure even in a hardened and wounded heart. It needs to be released from the things that confine and hide it so the potential to give life and delight can be utilized. The treasure must be freed from the entrapping structure of pain and mind-set of oppression that have kept the heart's treasure unseen and locked away. Those who would care for the soul/spiritual heart of My children need to have the heart to do the careful labor. They need to understand the importance of a gentle but firm exposure and search. These practitioners of heart surgery must have the wisdom and obedience to cut gently and then to submerge the heart in living water before opening the heart to expose the contents. As the careful probing search takes place, the debris which held the treasure of the heart locked away will float to the surface for removal. The treasure will sort out from the agents of confinement. The hands of the surgeon will be clean and the treasure exposed will be washed in the living water ... made ready for immediate use or stored away until its chosen time.

Stop ripping apart the hearts of the wounded, diseased, and confined in your unwashed hands, My child. Stop throwing

71

out the treasure with the debris in your urgency to obtain and, in your frustration, to complete the laborious task. Those who are not anointed, called, and trained to do this vital work must cease from participating in it. Instead, offer up your own heart for harvesting, so that you will be usable to harvest the hearts of others; bringing them wholeness and release. Your stained hands give evidence to your lack of understanding of the process and the preciousness of what you touch.

I long for the hearts of My children to be made whole. Too long I have seen the disease and wounding that has come to these hearts through the painful darkness of a fallen world. Even as the high priest in ancient days carried the symbols of the hearts of My people on his garments, so also does the final High Priest bear them. They are precious to Me. In a season yet to come, the hearts of all My children will be made totally perfect. There will no longer be a need for healing and repair. Until then, be aware of My love for the treasure I have placed with each of you. Call upon Me to bring it forth. Call upon Me to bring forth your healing and repair, and entrust this vital work only to those who have My life within them – only to those who have skill that has been given to them by Me.

As the treasure of your heart is harvested, and as you are released from all that confines your treasure, rejoice in Me. Celebrate the season of the pomegranate, knowing that it is I, little one, who carries your heart ever upon My own heart.

ONE PLUS ONE

Little one, I never intended for you to live alone. It was always My heart and design that I would share every moment of your life, for you to know deeply Who I am. My clear intention is also that you would have human companionship as well. There are times when a soul needs the experience of solitude; coming apart from other people to go more deeply into My embrace or to learn about himself. Sometimes discipline of the flesh requires one to withdraw from the surrounding comrades to make a personal accounting of one's heart and actions. However on a day-to-day basis, it was always My plan to have another of My children at your side. At times you will have many who fellowship with you and who join you in the journey. At other times one other person is sufficient. What is this sufficiency?

If you stood alone with a difficult decision to make, you would wrestle alone to consider the best course to take. With a companion you could consider the situation together allowing the perspective of one to confirm or to challenge the perspective of the other. Two people looking at the same scene can see two different sets of significant features and facts. There is less error if two seek My wisdom together to receive confirmation of the truth.

If you walked alone and fell into a deep crevice, who would hear your cry? Who would be nearby to see your plight and go for help? Who would be able to offer the help of a strong back, heart, and hands to pull you from your imprisonment?

If you were assigned a heavy burden to carry and discovered that it was too much for you to bear alone, the presence of another at your side could share the burden making it possible to fulfill the assignment.

If someone came to accuse you and to charge you falsely of wrongdoing, the person sharing your journey, walking at your side, could give accurate testimony of your location and actions at that moment of the supposed offense.

If you were walking alone and did not see the viper lying in wait on the road ahead, the eyes of your companion might be alert to the threat, warning you in advance of your next step. If by unhappy incident you were bitten by a viper on your journey, your companion would be able to give you aid and comfort. How difficult it would be to extract the venom from a bite by yourself!

If you walked up a narrow and dark path encountering a robber who grabbed you to harm you and to take your wealth, the assailant might be deterred from his intended assault if there were two of you. Your companion could rise up to defend you as you join together in warfare to subdue and defeat the efforts of the thief.

When the entire world refuses to hear your voice or to extend love and grace when you fail, as all will do at times, your companion on the road will be for you the word of truth, the assurance of your value, the encouragement for your heart to push back the defeat and pain.

If there was a deadly spider descending a thread of her web just above your head, you, as you sit all alone, would be unaware of the danger. A companion at your side would see the threat and knock down the spider to crush its attack before being completed.

If there was the beginning of a cancerous growth arising on the skin of your back, without a companion to observe what was out of your sight, you would be unaware of the threat until the growth had established deep and deadly roots. Such an observation as would be made by your companion could easily save your life.

If sorrow and grief were to consume your soul in an hour of deep loss, if fear caused you to curl into a terrified tight ball, the enwrapping arms of your companion could divide your grief as it is shared. The embrace of your fellow traveler on the road of life could reassure you of the truth that you are not alone as the courage of one restores the faith, hope, and courage of another.

There are so many possibilities and blessings that come with one plus one walking together. Facts are established, prayers are made in agreement, threats are averted, comfort is given, wisdom is shared …

Because of these blessings arising from two journeying together, the enemy of the flock works very hard to break up pairings. His strategies are many and they are vile. Too often they are successful. I want you to be aware of these things, so that you avoid being pulled apart in your purposeful companionship by the father of lies.

The chief means used to break up the fellowship of companions is pride. It seeks to raise up the significance of one person while challenging the right of the other to hold any authority in the relationship. Let me explain.

Satan *hates* holy unity. He hates the agreement of love and servanthood. If one companion is given the impression that he is sufficient of himself, not really *needing* another one to add to his life, there is a tendency to see the other person as unnecessary. The message is given that it is a weak thing to need another person – that there is a higher value in being self-sufficient. Soon an estrangement occurs; often fueled by the lie that two are not better than one, rather, that one is superior. But what if the one you are refusing is the very one that I sent to bring you the pieces you need to prosper in the journey?

This kind of thinking opens the door for the next lie – believing that somehow one person will be robbed by the strength within the other. It is as if there is a definitive amount of truth and authority for which the two must contend. If all the authority is deemed to be the right of one person, surely he will interpret shared authority as taking away a portion of what is rightfully his.

Consider the case of making decisions based on the counsel and wisdom of the two companions. The two hold opposing opinions. Each person believes his way to be the wisest course. The deceptive line of thinking goes on to suggest that if the first was to compromise his stand, yielding up a portion of his conclusion, thus allowing for a portion of the opinion of the second person to be valid, the first could be seen as personally losing ground to the second. Satan constantly presses upon this inclination within My children to win and excel over another person. The goal for the discussion has ceased to be the decision at hand, switching to become a contest of personal power of one over the other. Such behavior brings death into the unity of a relationship. Will not both win and prosper if the portions of wisdom deposited in each would join together to form a solid and unified solution based on confirmed wisdom from Me?

Foolish little one, if the substance of deepest value within you is truly Me, it would be impossible for someone to steal that treasure from you. Likewise, it would be impossible for you to rob that portion of Me, contained within another of My children, to accomplish your own gain. There is only destruction to the relationship and to the Kingdom as you seek to deprive each other of what is essential, in order to cause loss in one to promote yourself. The problem comes from your ownership of things that are not yours to possess, but rather only yours to use as I direct. Are you so unsure of your value and authority that you need to flex your muscle in these areas at the cost of peace and truth between you? You will build nothing that will endure unless you allow My gifts within each of you to prosper to the fullest level. Stop competing with each other and begin to rejoice in the abundance I have placed in your companion. The abundance is there to bless and to increase both of you, as well as the world in which you live.

How can the two of you ever walk together in peace and in prosperity unless you first agree on the fact that you are not in competition for anything. How can you ever hope to build up the Kingdom if you are given over to building up your own position in the relationship I have established between you?

The only thing weaker than the power of one in total isolation is two tearing apart things that were meant to bring forth the expressions of the Kingdom of God.

I give to you a word of caution now, little one. Be certain that the one you are walking with is one I have chosen for you. The ease of the journey together does not necessarily verify My choice and blessing upon a pairing. You can journey with another person on a soul level, managing to journey comfortably and successfully for a time. Comfort and the successful meshing of souls do not necessarily indicate prosperity. The presence of holy fruit in the relationship does indicate the presence of blessing. Sometimes precious Kingdom fruit will come forth out of times of difficulty in a relationship. Often false fruit comes out of comfortable soul bonds. You must know the difference. You must know My choice for you in order to prosper in truth and in blessing.

I have given you many reasons to walk with your human companions in unity with My purposes. I have cautioned you about the hazards of walking in a way that I have not ordained for you. The thing that I want you to know most of all concerning the journey with a companion is this: Always take Me with you. I must be your first and foremost companion even in the presence of your human companionship. The benefits that I shared with you of having another to walk alongside of you on the journey are benefits that I perpetually offer to you. I will help you in times of trouble. I will lift you up when you fall. I will free you from your prison. I will warn you of threats on the road. I will heal and comfort you. I will battle your enemy. I will bring you truth in decision making and courage in the midst of your fear. I will safeguard your health. I will always listen to your heart and hold it with the utmost of care. I am your best and most faithful companion. Just because I have also given you human companionship does not mean that I have set you aside from journeying with Me. You and I together – One plus one – is a great delight to Me and a great safeguard for you. Do not seek to journey with members of the flock while leaving behind the Shepherd. The attack of the devouring enemy awaits such a move.

One plus one is the foundational mathematics for One plus two, One plus three, One plus four, and so on. *One* is the foundation. Adding yourself to the foundation makes Kingdom multiplication a certainty and Kingdom subtraction only a lie.

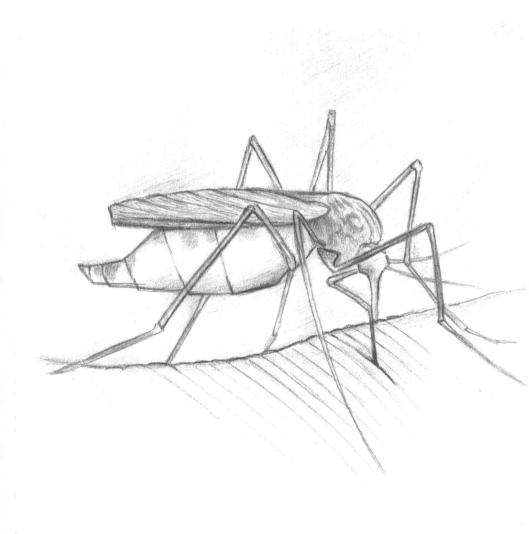

OPPORTUNISTS

Little one, listen as I again speak to you of My Kingdom's treasure. I speak of the anointing of blessings, gifting, and calling that I ordained for you to receive and to use for both enriching the world and honoring Me. To each of My little ones I impart a unique expression and combination of these treasures. I created each one of you to be individually special, carrying unique and individual treasure. Troubles arise when My selected impartations given to each one become the focus of comparison, envy, and competition within the hearts of My children. Why would I choose to give generously to one and sparingly in that same area to another? Why would I give many endowments to some and fewer to others? This matter of individual abundance is never to be your concern. I lovingly determine these things for My purposes. I assign them out of My wisdom, not out of your biased assessment. If this is not understood and if the human standards of equality are applied to My decisions, I am reported as being unfair. In their offense, the jealous ones seek to overthrow My determinations. They look for opportunities to contradict and to decry My blessing within another, seizing these things for themselves. They call for human considerations and evaluations to be applied to what I have ordained, so that they will create the opportunity to take what is not theirs to have.

Have you noticed how the mosquito lusts for the lifeblood within your body? I have allowed him to be a living example of an opportunist hovering to seize what is not his to possess. He is not content to have his own life, but takes the lifeblood of others in order to acquire stolen substance for himself – to prosper his own life.

The mosquito is hatched upon standing water having no movement upon its surface. He spends his life flying about looking for an opportunity in which to feed, uninvited, upon fresh blood. The lustful mosquito waits for one of My children to enter into his arena. He looks for a patch of uncovered skin to be the vulnerable site for his attack. Often he will hover on the ceiling or out of range until you quench the light of your room to go to sleep. If he waits to make his attack after you are in deep rest, he can dine freely without interruption or defense. Due to his small size he would be unnoticed in his advance, if not for the sound of his buzzing wings. I have caused these wings to be a warning sign for your ears to hear. If you are distracted by louder noises, or if your ears are covered, you may not hear his approach. Before you are aware of his presence, the mosquito's light weight body settles on the surface of the skin, penetrating it, injecting it, and then sucking out a measure of your blood.

He flies away satisfied with his acquisition, feeling justified that he left a measure of his own fluid within you to replace what was rightfully his to take. You are left enduring the swell and itch confirming the deposit of his substance and his theft of yours. In some cases, what he leaves within you is more than an itch. At times he leaves behind, within your body, a virus, bacteria, or a parasite. Over time the cost to you for his invasion can be very dear. Not only did he steal a small measure of your blood, but your health and your function as well.

Consider these things now as they apply to opportunists among you, little flock.

Jealousy, competition, and theft of My treasure given to you is hatched where there is still water. Where living water is moving these things cannot breed and arise. Holy things are born where there is a flow of living water. The unholy arises from the stagnant.

Do not spend your life lusting for the life that I have placed within another of My own children. Do not view what is within others as your entitlement. To do so is to see and to evaluate what they have through your human standards of fairness. Discontentment is an egg that hatches into jealousy when you see through these eyes.

Be careful as you journey together not to hover in lust over another one's anointing, calling, or opportunity. Journey together. Glean from the deposit that I have put within the mind, heart, or spirit of another as that one offers it up to you. Share your specific deposit of treasure with others.

As you journey together you will see the weak and vulnerable places found in all of My anointed children. Do not use your position of nearness to be a place from which you launch an attack upon those exposed areas. Do not seek to find places of frailty in another to be compared to your strength or you will be tempted into pride.

Do not use the power of your high position or your freedom of movement to take advantage of other members of the flock. Do not conceal yourself and your inner, unholy motives, but rather confess and reject those inner inclinations to rob and to wrongly use the confidence you have been given.

Never inject the substance of slander, doubt, suspicion, or gossip into one of My honored little ones, as you seek to dilute their treasure to take some honor for yourself.

Be aware that what you leave behind is often more than discomfort and incidental loss. You may bring forth weakness, pain and sickness, transferable to many, as you rob and replace wholeness with the fruit of your jealousy.

Most of the time the discomfort brought on by the bite of a mosquito is brief. However, sometimes it brings long-term chronic suffering or acute illness with death. It is the same with jealousy, competitive attacks, and theft against My chosen ones. You may take lightly the loss from a mosquito bite. I never take lightly loss enacted against one of My little ones from another member of the flock.

Take note, you, to whom much has been given. Be aware that your selection may cause those of insecure standing to arise in jealousy and in competition against what I have entrusted to you. Do not expect that attacks will come, but always be alert to the sound of buzzing wings. Do not be so absorbed in what you are doing that you miss the alerts of unrest and dysfunction that are beginning to arise against you. Do not let these things deter you from your assigned task nor take you off course, but neither let them be ignored. Address the potential for attacking mosquitoes by confronting the lies that breed and nurture the eggs of discontent and comparison in the stagnant water of another's life.

The way of the mosquito is the way of the opportunist. The way of the opportunist is the way of My enemy. Come out of your inclination to decide what is yours to have or to take, little one. Receive, rejoice, and honor what I have determined to be your endowment as well as the endowment of others. Be content with what I have given to you, so that jealousy and competition will not have a place to take root in your heart. Give generously to others in the flock, seeking nothing for yourselves other than what I have given to you. In this way you will add to the lives of each other, and in doing so will add to My Kingdom.

To operate as a mosquito in the midst of My flock will deplete it and yourself as well. Focus instead on giving rather than taking – giving a blessing rather than seizing one, giving honor rather than depriving one of honor, opening up opportunities to others rather than hoarding them or creating them for yourselves. Remember, those who dwell in My Kingdom are not living to gather in glory for themselves. My precious ones seek only to give glory to their Shepherd, whose lifeblood flows through them.

SELF-TRUTH

So, little one, you have asked Me to tell you about yourself. You are seeking after self-truth? It pleases Me that you would seek after this knowledge – too few wish to know these things.

Shall I reveal to you those truths about you which I have seen? Little one, in your years since youth, you have come to know and to delight in the approval, and in the appreciation of others. You are truly loved by Me, but often that must be confirmed in your mind by the love of others shed upon you as well. Most often, you present yourself to the world in loveable ways. My goodness is in you. But the flesh that still rules the corners of your life needs to be addressed too so that your fullness in spirit might come forth.

You are right to recognize that you have come from a competitive, judgmental, and prideful lineage. You war against it, and yet it remains. I have seen you consciously reject these inclinations at times, and at other times, they are allowed to move freely through you and out of you to strike upon others.

You have high expectations. These are very good, if they are Mine. If, however, you impose your own expectations upon yourself or upon others, you will create difficulty, as they are unmet.

Too often I see you quick to interpret the actions of others, to label them, to classify them, and to store them away for later use. They can become for you a quick reference and index to the flaws of others. I have seen you resist this flesh, refusing to act in accordance to this tendency many times, and yet the predisposition to store up records concerning the weaknesses of others remains.

All My little ones love to be loved. You who have come to know Me, love to be loved first and foremost by Me. However, each of you still loves to have the love of others whose skin you can touch and whose affirming embrace can enwrap you. That is good. It pleases Me greatly to establish you in loving human relationships. And yet, there are times when this latter aspect of your love requirements, becomes a stumbling block. To retain another's love and admiration, you can be given over to compromising truth, suiting it to the need you see before you. You may be inclined to set truth aside to hold onto a relationship which affirms you and which meets an inner need. Little one, truth must never be compromised or laid aside or falsehood will enter in to rob you of the deeper blessings brought by truth in relationships.

As a person who draws from My strength, you are seen as strong and worthy of admiration. That feels pleasant to you. You are less inclined to show your weaknesses to others, because in the eyes of the world there is less honor there. It greatly honors Me to hear from your heart the confession of your weaknesses. In this confession you are left vulnerable to

My forgiveness, remaking, and healing. This is not so with the world.

To tell your weaknesses to the world is to leave yourselves vulnerable to ridicule and to abuse. And yet the world will need to see My strength in you, through the overcoming of your weaknesses by My love and abilities. It is a courageous and generous thing to humbly show your weakness to a struggling world which thinks itself to be strong and powerful. However in the same breath that you speak of your weaknesses, you must speak of My power in you to overcome them. I do not want My little one, designed for victory, walking the earth giving a testimony of reigning defeat and dysfunction.

The world is filled with people who need My strength in you. That is why I have made you strong in Me. Others who are fragile, measure their weakness against your strength, and evaluate themselves in their inner hearts to be less by comparison. Often they rise up in anger or in jealousy, not wanting to be reduced in their own eyes or in the eyes of others. They may crawl into self-pity or despair. Are you to blame for their challenging and hurtful responses? Most often you are not. However, do you ever solicit them? If you consider this question honestly, you would have to admit that in a moment of irritation or in a moment of insensitivity toward the wounded rejected ones, you can be given over to your flesh, flaunting your strength before them. They have tried to create around themselves a world of honor and acceptance, which they do not know in their reality. Your reality of strength crashes down upon their paper house and upon their paper world, bringing their avoided reality into full view. Their response is anger, and yours is confused hurt.

How do you often respond to their wounded anger? Do you rise up with self-defense? Do you employ self-explanation to give witness to yourself? Does that help either the pain of the wounded one, or your own pain from being attacked? Where is your first focus? Is it upon Me? Do you come first to Me for insight, for wisdom, and for direction concerning the conflict? Do you see with compassion the place of pain in the other which you happened to touch? Are you more concerned with your own pain, and with the distorted view in which others may now see you as a result of this conflict?

What is your second response? Is it forgiveness, or do you cling to the words and to the memories, trying to reconcile them in some way? Are you able to walk away in My peace to seek a new path of understanding or to search for a doorway to healing for the wounds for the broken one? Where do you place blame for the incident? Who carries the invoice for the charges and payment due as a result of the offense? Do you pay part of it, or do you charge it entirely to the other person? Do you ever sacrificially pay for all of it? Even if rightfully it is not on your account, will you assume it all out of the love and grace that you have received from Me?

You will never have enough love of your own making to do these difficult things, little one. You must use My supply. You can never justify yourself, for I alone can justify you. Only the one with the authority to judge also has the power to justify. Who but I has the authority to judge?

You have come asking for self-truth, and I have served up a deep portion for you to consider. I do not speak of this accounting for any other reason than to draw you more deeply into Myself, and into My love. Truly I do delight in you. I see your heart long before I see your shortcomings. And I am patient with My little ones who lay themselves before Me to honor Me. I desire earnestly to form them into My dream of them. When you seek truth about yourself, let your first view be of one who is beloved and longed for beyond your understanding. Out of that truth will come the strength and the confident courage to submit to the refining truth necessary to deal with the weaknesses you have within. Hold these realities of My heart tightly, and use them as a bridge to bring many other imperfect, beloved little ones to find their strength and wholeness in Me.

PACIFIERS

Listen … do you hear a small baby crying? What disturbance to his peace or comfort causes him to cry out? Is his stomach demanding food? Could it be that his bottom is wet or dirty? Is he tired or is he lonely for a tight, reassuring embrace? Has the world suddenly seemed too big, too noisy, and too scary for him to now feel safe? If his needs to be cleaned, fed, or held are met by a loving caretaker, he may settle back into silence or into contented cooing to express his peace. At other times he may have had those immediate needs met, but there is still no peace within him. A frustrated caretaker may resort to putting a pacifier into his mouth to quiet him.

Consider with Me the realities of this pacifier, little one. Every baby is designed to have a desire to suck from his mother's breast to receive both his comfort and his food. This is an instinctive act with the purpose of sustaining the child's life. Those little babies who lack this instinct must be taught to draw comfort and food in this way or else alternative ways of feeding must be found quickly. When a baby has received the food and care that he needs, but does not realize these things while focusing on distractions around him, he may become agitated. The pacifier becomes a convenient substitute for mother's breast to comfort and appease him.

Some babies will eagerly receive the pacifier, while others see that it is false and reject it. Those who receive the device and suck contently upon it will settle into a temporary, contented state. Some find the pacifier so pleasing that it is difficult to get the child to abandon the internal comfort that it brings far beyond the years of infancy. These children will fight to keep a relationship with their pacifier becoming greatly agitated when it is lost to them, or when they are deprived of it.

Do you have pacifiers in your life, little one? Do you have substitutes for the nourishment and comfort that you were designed to draw from Me? What are these things that assure you of life and safety apart from Me? What is it that satisfies a need for stimulation and comfort other than Me?

Do you have religious practices – rituals and traditions that make you feel holy, but which do not necessarily make Me the focus of your actions nor give Me the honor?

Do you expound on doctrine and theory with an air of certainty to make you appear spiritually great against the insufficiency of your own mind and heart?

Do you fill your mouth with big words from big human thoughts to give you a bulwark against the fear of the unknown?

Do you have distractions from your stressful life which keep you from bringing your anxieties to Me for resolution and comfort? It is convenient to turn on your television set or to go to a movie to transport you into a world other than your own. You can live vicariously through the life of a character on the screen, rather than managing your own life with My guidance.

Do you use food to indulge the cry for comfort against the self-doubts and self-hatred you hold deep inside?

Do you nurse on the anger from wounds of the past to give you the power to live through each day of pain?

What are you addicted to as if it is a life-sustaining necessity to you? Whatever these things of pacification, artificial sustenance, and comfort might be, they will all fail you. When you are truly starving to death for true food, these false things will give you an illusion, not a reality of nourishment. They will lead you to death. When there is genuine threat surrounding you, sucking on your convenient and familiar pacifier will do little but give you a false sense of safety as you are overcome by the power of evil.

It is time that you grow up, little one. It is time that you put away the illusions arising from childish things. I have never left you comfortless. I have never left you without a rich supply of food. I have given you the truth of My Word and the presence of My surrounding Spirit to teach you the way of wisdom. You have not drawn from My source because your mouth has been too occupied by plastic satisfaction. You have not dined on My abundance because you have sought the abundance of the fallen world to comfort and to satisfy you. Confess these things of shallow pacification and lay them aside permanently.

Soon these pacifiers will be taken from you. I must do this for you to come out into maturity and into reality. You cannot remain in infancy. You cannot be allowed to cling to illusions, claiming them to be the realities which give you meaning, life, and security. Childish things must be put away. You will whine and protest. You may even despise Me and declare that I am harsh and uncaring. Yet, I will proceed with My intention for you, out of My great love for you.

Do not resist crying out to Me when you are in need. Do not fear the moments of inadequacy in yourself and in others. I know that these things are part of living upon the earth. I have the answers and the solutions you need to turn these moments into victory. Do not be self-conscious, holding your unsatisfied needs and fears hidden inside so that others will not think less of you. Be humble and simple like a child. Be transparent before Me and before others so that you will be a sign pointing to that which is real and enduring. Cry out and be truly comforted, truly fed, truly changed, truly embraced.

How I long for you to put these pacifiers aside by your own choice! How I long to fill your mouths with Myself and your bellies with the rich nourishment that arises from Me! I want you to be comforted with all true comfort, but I hate to see you deceived by the weak and false comforts of the world which I know will fail you. I am the provider of all good things. I give freely even as I love freely. Come draw near. Snuggle into My chest and drink deeply of all that I have to give you. I will not just pacify your needs, I will truly satisfy them.

STRETCHING YOUR NECK

———————————

Do you remember a time when you were very small and wanted to be taller? When everyone in the world around you seemed bigger than you, being short seemed like a great disadvantage. It also felt as if somehow you were less than others, rather than simply being shorter. You would stretch your body length to its maximum by rising up on your toes and by stretching your neck as far as you could. No matter how hard you tried, you could not maintain the extra inches temporarily gained. When the stretch was over, your real height remained the same as before.

Have you noticed that I created the vast variety of animals on the earth with a vast variety of shapes and sizes? Notice the differences in neck length. Why would that be an important distinction? What is on either end of the neck? Of course there is a head seated on one end of the neck, and a body of some form on the opposite end. The neck is really a connector between a head and a body. The neck is designed to function in concert with the head and the body. All are matched exactly in form and length to suit My purposes.

Without the neck, the head could not move about, turning to view what is to the side or behind the body. The head could not turn up or down without the neck. The head would have to depend upon the body to bend and turn to make up for the missing flexibility of the neck. Additionally, the neck serves as a conduit for the wiring running between the body and the head. If the connections of the neck are severed or broken, the function of the body is impaired or ceases altogether.

Do you ever consider the high value of the neck? Most only consider it a place from which to hang a necklace or a tie. Largely the neck is taken for granted until its function is impaired in some way.

Note the long neck of the giraffe. His diet consists of the high leaves of the trees. If he had a neck only as long as the turtle, he would starve. Consider the turtle. He is designed to eat from the foliage and life located on the ground and in the pond. What would he do with the neck of the giraffe? The length I assign to each neck has a specific purpose and function. These things did not arbitrarily develop over time as some might suggest. I created the human neck with just the right length and characteristics according to My plan, while at the same time standing as a reminder of the proper posture My children are to maintain before Me.

As with everything in the world, there is a spiritual connection and a parable of My Kingdom connected with the human neck. In addition to holding up the head, the neck is designed to support a yoke of burden along with the shoulders. In this way the neck becomes a sign of submission and servanthood. If the neck resists this calling, as suggested by a rebellious and proud heart, it is referred to as a stiff neck. It refuses to bend to the authority of another or to carry its assigned load. A stiff neck says that it will choose on its own what to do and when to do it. It will not accept being under authority, but chooses instead to be its own authority. This posture of heart is contrary to My design for your prosperity.

The neck is the symbol of the servanthood which is to be the way of your journey upon the earth. The neck serves both the head and the body. Consider this: if I am the head of authority and the body is the flock, what should your role be to both? My power running through you is to facilitate the function and movement – even the health of the body. Your flexibility and your humility allow My high vision to give information to the body from every direction. Without Me you have no function and neither does the Body. Unlike a severed human head, I can exist without either neck or body, but I have chosen both to be a part of Me.

Look to another parable. The neck supports your own physical head. It can cause your head to drop down to a lower position if you wish to hide your height and conceal your position. It can stretch just enough to allow you to see what is hidden above your eye level. In this way, your neck can raise or lower your head slightly according to a need or to your desire. If again the consideration is pride, think in this way: in the presence of someone struggling with his own insignificance in height, you are free to diminish your advantage by lowering your head or to exaggerate your position by increasing in loftiness. What is to be the posture of the servant?

There are times when I place you in great authority over others. Are you willing to be the servant leader who yields to

My yoke and who does not bring attention to the position I have given you in order to gain honor for yourself?

There are times when I will place upon your neck an uncomfortable or an inconvenient burden of assignment. Will you bow to receive it and with joy carefully carry what I have placed upon your shoulders; or would you stand up against My will for you, refusing to receive the yoke?

Are you content to be exactly as I have created you for My purposes, or do you try to determine your course by the appetite of your own desires and by operating out of your own assumed abilities?

I need humble little ones to walk closely with Me, doing My bidding with receptive and submitted hearts. Will you choose to be one of these soft, strong necks in My service? Will you try to stretch yourself, extending your neck to bring your head above others? If you lift your own head, know that I will be unable to lift it for you. If you choose to have your own head and to exalt it yourself, you will never know the blessing of My hand under your chin raising your face up to meet Mine. You will never know the delight of My hand raising your head above those of your enemies. You will never know the deep honor that comes from Me, given to a submitted heart in My service.

If you have a desire to lead, but neither the calling from Me nor the gifting from Me, you will suffer the pain of a stiff neck as you pursue a position I have not established nor designed for you. You will be the turtle who believes himself to be a giraffe. His efforts will be expended trying to stretch his neck to reach the trees, while he starves for the lack of food.

Be exactly who you are called to be, little one. It is enough to be splendid in My design. It is enough to be a servant neck, so the true head can be exalted and the body can function in strength. Your position is secure and it is marvelous. Now, little one, bend your neck before Me … not to receive a yoke from My hand, but in this moment to receive a loving kiss from My lips to your head.

TAKING OFFENSE

How quickly My children, even My own called by My name, are given to possessing offense. They take offense, they assume it, and they harbor it in their hearts, often retaining it within their memories for years. It may begin as a word of insult, a sideways glance, an insensitive action, or even as a face turned away. Each careless or misinterpreted word and action can be owned as a personal assault by My fragile children. Motives and the intentions can be so easily assumed, if they are not made clear or explored together. Injury and anger can set up a wall around an offended place of the heart so it becomes impenetrable to the oil of forgiveness and reconciliation. Any truth concerning the realities of a relationship often becomes clouded behind a flow of steam born out of anger and hurt.

Why are you so quick to take up offense, and then to keep it – even sharing it with others? What is it that you need to protect, or to uphold by this posture of your heart and mind? Is it not a matter of your self-image and personal, situational view which you are seeking to defend? Is it not your own self-evaluation being challenged?

What are the thoughts that flood your mind as you consider the potential of an offense being thrust upon your soul? "Who does he think he is?" Is this not a measurement in comparison to who you think you are? "What makes him think that he knows better than I?" "What rights does she assume over mine?" Are these things not most often a clash between you and another concerning what you believe you know, of what you believe to be your right to do or to have – even a clash with what you believe you deserve? Are these not the things of your soulish *self* in conflict with another?

These evaluations of self run deeply throughout the human soul. These tendencies in my little ones to draw lines of determination, boundaries of self-influence, and indicators of injury are well practiced. Where do they come from? These things of offense most often arise out of an insecure evaluation of personal worth and of self-value. It is as if the self is a fragile treasure of limited quantity, which must be carefully guarded from theft by others. Is that who I created you to be? Is that who you are?

What is the treasure within you? Did I not deposit within you great treasure intended to be given away and also to be made available to others? Who can steal what is My own? Who can deplete what I am continually increasing?

These questions call you to a deep place, little one. They call you to a reality apart from the world's understanding. How often have you heard the terms, "self-made, self-assured, self-confident, and self-sufficient"? You see the world exalts the *self*. The identity, the value of the person, is seen to be the self. To the world the treasure of the self is established in the soulish qualities of human emotion, will, and intellect. How far this is from My reality of the treasure I established within My human creation! My children have their identity and value established in Me. It is My presence with them. It is My handiwork through them. It is My life imparted within them that has made their human substance a treasure. This treasure was designed to be poured out to others, even as My life flowing through them was designed to be endless.

I have called My children of truth to walk and to live in this understanding which I have laid before you. Have you not heard that you are called to die to yourself? To do so means that you embrace the truth of life in Me. I am abundance. I am unlimited. I am all wisdom. I am all compassion. I am perfect forgiveness. If you have too much of yourself stored up as valued treasure, you will have little room to contain what I am. Your presence of self overshadows My presence, and crowds it out, by your own choice. When you have become the priority of your own life, you have chosen yourself, over Me. Do you understand that? You have moved Me aside, taking My place, while placing your perceptions and desires over and above My truth and over My desires. If you are fully alive in yourself, and not walking within My life, you will have perpetual conflict. The self in others will offend the self in you. Your self of flesh is easily bruised, as it is weak and fragile against the world. It is easily influenced by the things of darkness. Injury adheres tightly to the substance of human self. These things are precisely why it must whither and die.

There must not be a struggle of the flesh in control within the fellowship of My true, precious children. My Spirit alone must be in control of any community declaring My name over it. There must not be injured self, injuring others – those acting like cells of a human body attacking others of its own cells within it. There must be continuous dying to self even as there must also be continuous healing of all of My children who are called to walk together before Me and before the watching eyes of the world. Eventually all human flesh will die. Would it not be better to live in the eternal now, rather than to allow that which will surely die, to continue to rule in your hearts and minds?

If I am the life operating within My children, then they shall live in peace. As you live out of that which the world values, the flesh of one will arise to conflict, to control, or to compete with the flesh of another. This is the way of the world of flesh. But to those who, even now, live out of My Spirit, My presence alive within My children can absorb and assume any offense raised against them. Consider this: which feels the pain of a needle? Is it the skin that is alive, or skin that is dead? After a severe burn, the top layer of skin will die. Which layer of skin then feels the pain? Is it the dead that is peeled away, or the new life under it which cries out for relief?

That skin of your self which has been submitted to My refiner's fire has died. It is peeled away. The new life, My presence alive within you, will be impacted by the pain of an offense. It will absorb it, even as My healing power over the injury was already established and put into effect nearly 2,000 years ago. Since I am eternal, no injury will destroy the new creation within you. The parts of your flesh which have not been yielded up to death are the areas which will be impacted by the pain of offense and which will absorb it. Whether arising from true offense or from wrongly assumed offense, these areas of perpetuated injury can become infected by other soulful invasions, bringing a sickness of soul and a deterioration of the true treasure within you.

Whenever you feel the pain of offenses made against you, little one, look to see what is yet alive of the old nature. See to your pride. See your control. See your self-determination. See how much you prize and defend your own understanding. Humility brings the death of pride. Humility is the substance of abundant life, while pride is the substance of decay and loss. This truth applies to every relationship – even to your relationship with Me.

If I am who is in control of your life, who then could threaten your fulfillment? If I am the Source of all your understanding, who could ever deprive you of truth? Are you so unsure that truth will live forever? Do you believe that it will die unless you support its life with the addition of your own human understanding of truth? Yes, I call you to speak truth, and to defend it against falsehood. And yet, I am the only Source of this defense. Rather than mustering your own weaponry, use Mine. If My truth is alive in you, it will flow, and it will suffice – even if the one attacking will not receive it.

Too many of My children assume their opinions to be truth. When these things move and shift, as assumptions do, My children often try to shore them up with more of their own reasoning. It then becomes a continuing battle with others, and with the opinions of others. This type of soulish encounter becomes the substance out of which many occasions of offense will arise. Speak truth in humility, and then let it live and move as I choose. Do not try to pump more power or more validity into My truth, by adding your own perspective on it. Let My truth quietly stand. Allow yourself to quietly stand within that truth, as I defend it and you for speaking it.

So many of your conversations are self-focused, rather than focused upon Me. As a result, you experience many opportunities for offense and conflict. Much of your focus and vision is made up of self-perspective rather than Mine, to the point that you have trouble seeing past yourself to

My purpose, as it is alive in the journey of another one of My children. Allow the journey of each of My little ones to be his or her journey individually with Me. Do not presume to impose what has been the substance of your journey, causing it to crash down upon that which I am doing with others. If you do not heed this instruction, you can become a hindrance to My fullness in others, and a distraction from what I have in store for you.

No one can walk upon this earth without conflict, for truly there are two kingdoms in conflict throughout the world. But it is possible for my true children, alive in Me and dead to self, to live and walk in peace with each other. The things of My Kingdom have become the focus and the priority of the lives of those who live together in peace. If My presence within them is the source of all life and truth, they find agreement with each other. If My truth is the foundation of their lives, a time of healing and restoration will follow every clash and challenge between them, as they submit their flesh to that truth.

Look to your level of disharmony and offense. What is there that still needs to die within you so that My grace and My life might spring forth in abundance? Whatever of your soulish self is still alive in your flesh, it will deny life and forgiveness to the lives of others. See to these things in yourself – not to these things in others. Your accounting is your own before Me. See to those things of self in your own charge, and not to that accounting in others. You truly cannot bring about a holy death of the flesh within another person. You would only be able to bring about unholy destruction. Invite My presence in you to bring about your own death of self; and then watch My presence in your reborn life be used to bring about new life in others.

WOUNDED PUPPIES

How wonderful it is to have a young puppy in your arms! The joy of life overflows from a healthy puppy, consuming everything around him. His little body cannot contain all the energy and excitement. It must be in constant motion to relieve the great pressure of new life bubbling up within him. The puppy must bark, chew, lick, and run until the moment of total exhaustion sets in. Then suddenly the puppy curls into a ball or stretches out in the sunshine and falls off into a deep sleep. Even in his sleep he runs and barks in his delight to be alive.

Puppies are so fresh and new, and also so immature. There is so much that they must learn if only they can stay focused long enough to receive the lessons. Puppies have great trouble with boundaries. The whole world beckons them to see and taste deeply of new experiences. Puppies must learn. They must learn what is safe. They must learn what their master requires of them. It may take a bit longer for the master to see the results of training lessons, but over time the evidence of understanding and maturity will come. The playful nipping, and recreational chewing on unacceptable items during puppy-hood, will be replaced by appropriate biting upon special doggie toys in maturity. Incessant barking will soon be replaced by a bark of alarm or surprise. In time, house training will be complete, eliminating the misplaced puddles and piles on the floor. Still, long after puppyhood is left behind, there will be a puppy's heart, even in an aged dog.

You, little one, have much in common with puppies. When you are fresh and new to the world and able to move about, you too are filled with energy and curiosity. Boundaries are things for which you have no concept. The call of the flesh makes it difficult to attend to the instructions of your Master. At first, everything must go into your mouth for exploration, or for appetite satisfaction. At first, your cry is the only communication. As time passes, and as maturity increases, you begin to communicate with words. Exploration through touch joins in concert with deliberate reasoning of the mind. When you mature, you are obedient to discipline and instruction, practicing both in order to delight your Master.

The way from immaturity to maturity is My way for both you and for the puppies of the world. Sometimes the process of maturing is more difficult than at other times. Often you express a resistance to the learning and to the boundaries that have been set for you. Rebellion against restrictions arises out of immaturity and inhibits the onset of maturity. Sometimes the consequences to rebellion are slight and sometimes they are severe. It is My will that rebellion would depart from you, so that in your maturity you would be safe and prosperous in all that I assign to you.

Listen now as I tell you about wounded puppies – those rebellious little ones vulnerable to harm. Someone needs to confine puppies when they refuse to ignore the warnings of danger, and go running into the street during a mindless romp or rebellious impulse. Fences help them stay safe. Tethering keeps them confined at a safe distance from the traffic of the road. Sometimes, the puppy will wait for a moment when the fence is open or when the door is ajar. Sometimes he will bolt quickly and suddenly toward the street when the lead is disengaged.

Sadly there are times when a puppy will run out into the path of a vehicle on the road and become wounded. The sound of his cry is heart-rending. He is in pain and in terror. These sensations of agony are new to him. His inability to move or to get up and run away brings terror to his heart. He is helpless and frightened. What help is there for the wounded puppy lying in the midst of the roadway?

Who will venture into the street to rescue the puppy before the next vehicle comes along? This is a very important question for you to consider – not just as it relates to wounded puppies, but also pertaining to My wounded, human, little ones.

It takes the heart of someone with great love for the puppy to dash out into the street to rescue him. It takes someone of great courage, even if there is no speeding traffic to threaten the rescuer. A strange thing happens in the mind of a wounded, helpless puppy. He knows only one thing – he is in pain. In his immaturity he has a lack of clarity concerning the source of his pain. He is unable to see that venturing out of his safe boundaries made him vulnerable to the threat. He is unable to recognize the fact that the vehicle, which struck him, is the reason for his pain. He knows only one thing – he is in pain and any movement makes the pain worse.

When his brave and loving rescuer comes to scoop him up lovingly in his arms, the puppy will bite and violently protest. The pain in his body is credited to the one moving him and helping him to safety. To rescue a wounded puppy, to prevent a more deadly blow, to get help for the wounded one, means that someone must be willing to endure the bites. Someone must be willing to have his skin torn and his heart torn by the puppy's misguided attack while in pain. To stand back from making the rescue attempt, in fear of being hurt, gives death a chance to crush the life from the puppy.

Often My human children have wandered beyond where they need to be. Sometimes out of rebellion, and sometimes out of curiosity, immaturity, or a sense of fun, they run out into a place of great danger. Pain comes to them as something in life's roadway knocks them down, injuring them. They sit or lay in the middle of the road crying out in dysfunction and in pain. Their behaviors are erratic, their choices are poor, and their mood is self-defensive. To stay where they are is deadly, but they have no sense of that reality. They only want instant and complete relief, so they can continue on. They are in pain but the immaturity of their understanding of spiritual and natural consequences keeps them from having the clarity of why they are in that deep pain.

If someone of sacrificial love risks the hazards of extending care, of moving the wounded ones from the place of threat, in order to bring them to a place of healing, those receiving the love often snarl and bite their rescuer. They credit the pain they are feeling to the one who is moving them out and away from the road they are on. They blame. They slander and decry the helper who has been sent by Me to bring them out of the pain and threat. Often these wounded ones protect their wounds, not allowing them to be seen or touched, as if doing so makes their condition less real. Sometimes they deny the pain of being struck and credit their condition entirely to being moved or handled. Just like a child who screams at a parent for removing an infected splinter from a hand, as if the parent is the source of their pain and problem, so also do My children in pain of the soul respond to those sent to help them.

Immaturity does not want to see its role in a present problem, whether it is immaturity in the wounded puppy or the wounded human being. Self-protection becomes the priority of the heart. Do not see … do not touch … do not move – these are the commands from the immature heart in pain. Wisdom cannot speak the truth to them. Love and care are seen only as problematic. Those who want to hide their wounds, wanting to continue crawling around in the roadway as if they are only temporarily delayed, are in the greatest danger. They bark, "Stay away from me. I can handle this situation. Don't suggest that I have a problem requiring me to change course or to come to anyone for help. You are responsible for my pain!"

Long before you knew that you were in pain, I, your Shepherd, saw the reality of it. In My great love for you I chose to enter into the roadway of life to pick you up in your wounded and dysfunctional state. My heart was to spare you from the threat of death that was surely heading your way to crush you. So many of you have bitten Me and snarled at Me. You have decried Me to others and charged Me with being the source of your pain and circumstances. You are too immature to understand the role you played in coming to your broken and painful condition. But still, I continue to lift you up and I move you because I love you. I am willing to do what is necessary to save you, while waiting for a time when you will fully understand the truth of your life and of My role in preserving it.

Likewise, I see many of you damaged little ones crawling around on the roadway of life in need of human help. I send My servants to lift you up and to bring you to a place of healing. Instead of receiving their love and Mine, which has come to you through them, you bite and accuse; you slander and you decry them. Both your immaturity and your pain rise up against holy help and the truth that must come with it. The illusions are a safe hiding place away from reality and responsibility. Staying on the defensive keeps My servants from getting too close, where they might see realities about your life that you would prefer to remain unseen. If you raise up enough threat, making the cost so great to them, perhaps they will leave you alone, you surmise. Ah, but then you do not really know Me, nor My true servants. As I am willing to risk pain so that you might be made whole, so also have I raised up servants of My own heart to do the same.

It's time that the puppies grow up into a new maturity. It's time to see clearly the real source of threat and pain. It's time to look through the eyes of truth at the rebellion that brought you to this state and at the pride which keeps you in it. The days are becoming more hazardous upon the roadway of life. Those who refuse My help and the help of the servants I have sent, may soon be casualties.

Little one, you have been called by Me to go to those in pain and delusion, to those who are wrapped in self-protection and pride – so you must prepare for a great work upon the earth. You must come more deeply into My heart to acquire the needed courage and strength of love. Soon the world will be filled with wounded human puppies wailing in pain and in need of rescue. Will you be willing to sacrifice your hands and your heart to the tearing bite of the wounded, so that you can move them to a place of safety? Will you be willing to reset the bones that are broken even as they beat upon you in rage as if you are the source of their pain and trauma? You must count the cost – both to yourself in this service, and also to the threatened wounded ones if you would refuse to serve.

This is a heavy thing I ask of you. I only ask this of those who love Me and who care for the concerns of My heart. Be faithful and courageous, not expecting the thanks of the ones you gather up in your arms. My thanks to you will be the joy of your heart in this life and in the next. Do not fear. Run to gather up the wounded as I call out to you the assignment.

Know this: I am your sufficiency in this task. The love you will bear into the roadway of life will be Mine within you. The courage you take with you will arise from the heart of a lion. The wounds you suffer will be absorbed into the wounds I have suffered as you release your pain to Me for healing.

When this life is past, so also will the wounds and the threats be past. There will be no more immaturity and no more rebellion. Then all My divinely mature children will be as fresh, precious puppies, delighting in everything surrounding them to the fullness of joy. This life of freedom and delight will be unending. I promise.

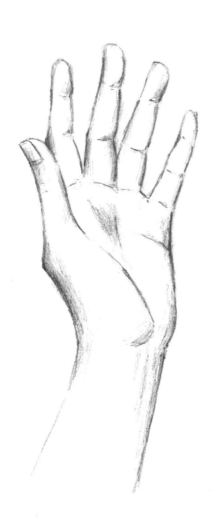
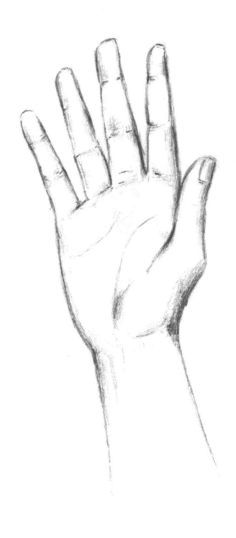

THROW UP YOUR HANDS

What is it, little one, that can come upon you suddenly, or perhaps develop slowly, which can cause you to feel overwhelmed? One minute you seem focused and confident. Your priorities are in proper order. Then, where you once had a firm grip upon My hand, something grips your heart giving you the impression that your life is no longer safe, on track, or manageable. You remove your hand to pick up your own life to manage it, at a time when you most need to cling to Me. Something happens to cause you to let go of truth, and with it, your shalom. What once was clear truth in your understanding becomes out of focus and uncertain. Ordered thinking becomes scattered. Trust, in My protection and in My sovereignty, is misplaced under a swirling storm stirred up by your mind and emotions. What is it that speaks more loudly to your soul than My promises? What is it that leads you to a place of crisis?

Often it is your own pride and self-will that moves upon your heart to capture your devotion, setting you up for a fall.

I know that you are fragile as you stand in your own strength and abilities. Do you remember Me reminding you to never depend upon yourself? In My strength you will always prevail, even in times when it feels that you are loosing a battle. Are you aware that I created you for victory and for joy, as well as for the purpose of love? If I created you for these things, would I not also supply you with everything that you need to be successful in every challenge? Pride and self-will suggest that you have within yourself a sufficient strength and a more perfect wisdom. These delusions cause you to lay aside My way and My instruction.

Children need to test their abilities as they grow. Sitting becomes crawling. Crawling becomes walking. Walking becomes running. In your life, I arranged for seasons of growth and new challenges to prosper that growth. When you have accomplished one milestone, I prepare you to achieve the next one. Step by step, under My guidance and tutelage, you journey through life. Sometimes, the pace of growth and the order of the steps that I have ordained do not meet with your approval. You see someone running while you are still walking, so you try to run before your development will allow success. You fall on your face. Defeat can quickly overwhelm you as embarrassment and frustration fill your heart. Disappointment, self-hate, and jealousy stand by, waiting for an opportunity to seize your peace and perspective. It is My heart that you would constantly be moving forward successfully with every new step. Your own heart presses you to undertake endeavors prematurely, and to go to places not prescribed, that eventually take you into the midst of a place of threatening defeat.

When you move ahead without Me, I always see the change of course that you make away from My path to fulfillment. Often I will watch your choices whispering hints of warning.

If you relentlessly ignore the hints, sometimes I need to take a watchful step back rather than to cordon you off within a place of wisdom and safety. There are times when children must learn by failure and frustration in order to know that they have made a poor choice. How painful it is to see one of My little ones continuously leave the path to find destruction, but then refuse to accept or to apply what they learn through their error.

A self-protected heart finds it difficult to admit to its sin. A stubborn heart has a priority of proving that its choices have been correct. Soon the error will be repeated – often with more pain and with more grave consequences. Eventually the heart will become overwhelmed as the circumstances demonstrate that there is no effective way to proceed in the chosen path. When the frustrated child sits down and cries out to Me, admitting defeat and error, then I can undertake to restore both the soul and the journey. When your rebellious heart moves away from Me, I eagerly await your return to begin your restoration.

Even as your own choices and pride can put you into places of hazard, where you will be overwhelmed, so also can fear. Whenever you leave My shelter of protection, by the influence of your own imagination or through the formation of your own conclusions apart from My Word, fear is quick to dictate your thoughts and conclusions. "What if" becomes the trigger to infuse your heart and mind with fear. What if the job providing my income is lost to me? What if my health fails? What if the people I treasure most abandon me? What if a dreadful war or a natural disaster comes into my world today? Such thoughts can quickly dissolve your peace, overwhelming you with the sense of vulnerability and threat.

Considering possible scenarios of loss and disaster tends to put My children into a mind-set of self-protection. In a moment of feeling overwhelmed they rush to do something to prevent that which they fear. Where is their shelter of safety? Where is their antidote for aging and eventual death? Where is the place to hide away from all the possible threats? Feeling pursued by that which overwhelms them, their minds race to discover a way out. They busy their hands as their heart rate increases. If only they could find the key, the answer to crush their fears by removing the possible threat that they dread so much. All the while the answer is standing nearby.

The answer is *Me.* I am the key. I am the hiding place. I am the antidote. I am the shelter. When you run to find *any* solution other than Me against whatever threatens your peace and safety, you will find only more uncertainty, failure, and fear.

Little one, I have great compassion for your weakness. You are weak, but I am mighty in strength. I understand your need to feel independent and grown up, but you were never designed to grow up without Me. The world was once a perfect and completely safe place for My little ones. However, the choice to disobey My voice and to reject My authority has made you vulnerable to loss and pain. Until the fullness of time has come, it will be this way. And yet, I did not leave you to walk the earth feeling overwhelmed and at risk while I washed My hands of you. My love never abandons the ones I love, even when I have been deeply wounded by their rejection of Me.

Even as My hand is mighty, so also is My love and faithfulness to shepherd you. You have the freedom to walk away and to sever the ties with Me. I, however, can only love while accepting your choice. I will see your painful moments of risk and loss arising from your rebellion. I will wait for you to come to the end of yourself. The heart will fail, the body will collapse, and the mind will be overwhelmed, but even in that state will you seek Me? The choice is yours to make.

In this life there will be times when you have no solution, no answer, no peace, and no comfort – except from Me. When frustration and failure make it impossible for you to take one more step, simply sit down. When fear and helplessness have you running in frantic circles, simply sit down. When your own solutions and answers have failed, and when the newspaper headlines prophesy disaster, simply sit down. When the physician's report tells you that disease has found a home in your body, and when relationships are broken beyond your ability to repair them, sit down. When your financial resources have dried up while demands and needs continue to rain down upon you, sit down. Sit down at My feet and listen for My perspective on these problems. Listen to My solutions, rather than taking things into your own hands and racing to manufacture your own remedies.

Little one, when you are overwhelmed in any way, regardless if the source is real or only anticipatory imagination, sit down. Stop running. Stop formulating. Stop digging and stop managing. Sit down and throw up your hands. Your hands are already weak and they are empty of anything valuable. Raise them up to Me. Your heart is weary and overburdened. Now, take your heart into your empty hands and yield it up to Me. As a little child, raise your hands up to your Daddy and simply say, "Pick me up Abba, I can't walk any further." With uplifted empty hands say, "I don't have the means or the way to fix things, Abba." When your heart is crushed with fear or with pain, simply say, "Carry me Abba, and hide me in Your arms."

You wait too long to throw up your hands, little one. You try to manage things, handling them, pondering them by yourself too long. Yield to My love and care. Yield to My instruction and leadership. In a posture of yieldedness, turn your hearts and minds away from pride, away from self-sufficiency, away from rebellious independence, and away from fear. Turn your eyes upward, away from your world and away from yourself. With empty hands uplifted, begin to praise and thank Me for all that I am already doing on your behalf, and to which you only need agree to receive. Stop struggling.

Throw up your hands in surrender and in praise. Watch the confusion, the panic, and the struggle give way to faith. Peace and confidence, truth and focus, order and understanding will return to you. I will again take hold of your hands to raise you up to My heart. Your eyes will behold the Eternal and the threatening temporal will fade in priority. You and I will again hold hands and we will walk together. In that moment of blessed reunion in strength, both of us will be overwhelmed … with love.

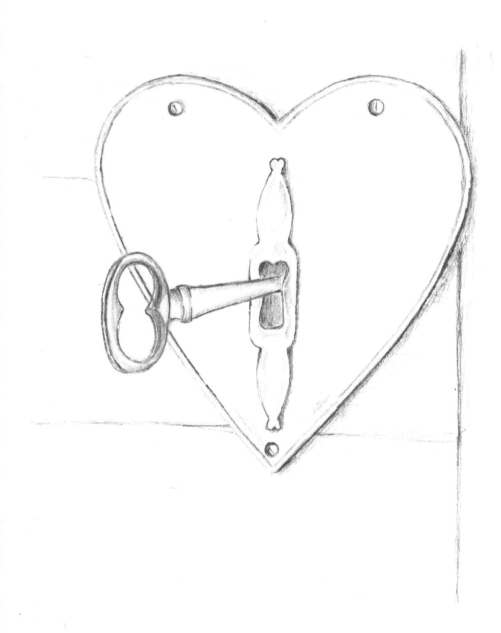

YOUR STOREHOUSE

Little one, what kind of storehouse have you created of your heart? Is that a silly question or a puzzling one for you? Consider this: your heart is to be the place of containment for many deep and important things, and a distribution center of these things as well. It would be good to know the nature of your containment vessel. That information will determine the type of substance it will safely be able to contain, as well as which things must never be stored there. For example, simple liquids can be stored in a water-tight container. Specific volatile liquids need a container that is not only water tight but also non-corrosive. At other times a storehouse allowing the breeze to blow through might be a vital requirement to keep the material contained within it dry and free.

So what is it that your heart is designed to contain? What kind of building material needs to form the structure of your heart to successfully contain them?

First and foremost, your heart was intended to contain a great abundance of love. Love is supposed to be a flow from Me to you, back to Me and on to others. In this case, your heart must have a large intake valve and a great output valve. To have one, while lacking the other, brings dysfunction. If I would pour great love into your heart, but you refused to pass it on, your heart would rupture and its contents would be lost altogether. If you had no intake valve but only an output, your heart would pour out love until there was no more. Your heart would become shriveled and small. You need a heart that is expandable and accommodating to all the love that I bring to you. At the same time you need one that has the ability to pour out that love, keeping a healthy and prosperous flow from you to Me, back to Me and on to others.

Have you noticed that I created your physical heart with this parable written into its function? Your heart of flesh was designed to be expandable and contractible. It receives blood and then passes it on to the lungs for refreshment and back out to the body to give health and strength. If the valves function well, the flow will be maintained if other features of the heart are also in health.

Besides love there are other things that I intend to flow through your storehouse heart. Generosity, kindness, mercy, compassion, and forgiveness are a few of these things. In each case they come from Me into your heart, where they are to be gratefully stored until I reveal to you an opportunity to pass on these things to others. When I say *"Forgive,"* the valve of your heart is to open, freely releasing forgiveness upon someone who has wounded you. If I say *"Show mercy,"* then you are to offer up mercy to the one I have revealed, even if your mind says that mercy is not deserved.

Beware of opening these valves when I have not called you to do so. Too many of My children operate in unsanctified mercy, offering generosity and opportunity to those prospering wickedness. In this way they provide an opportunity for evil to prosper against My call. You are never to give comfort to wickedness or to give it excuse and opportunity. You are never to extend kindness to lies and deception. Truth bears the signature of love when it is poured out to one in delusion and error, while not being delivered in a flow of angry human judgment. Your wisdom is insufficient in these things. Therefore, you must rely upon Me to direct both you and the flow from within your heart.

What are the things that you must never hold in your heart, nor ever pour out upon others? The fallen nature of the world brings with it much pain to impact your life. The mind responds and directs the heart to take in and to store things that I would not have you contain. Such things are bitterness, rage, condemnation, revenge, unforgiveness, pride, selfishness, etc. These are caustic substances to the human heart. The heart that I created in you cannot contain these things without deteriorating and ceasing to function. Therefore, to facilitate and to accommodate the storage and distribution of these volatile things, the mind will often create a different structure of the heart … not the one I designed for you.

Rather than being made out of living, expandable material, the human architect of the mind designs a structure made out of stone. The stony heart does not breathe. It does not beat in a flow of life, but rather is stagnant and dark. The caustic substances within it begin to etch grooves within the stony heart, creating an interior flow and mix of all these unholy substances. There are sharp edges to this storehouse of a heart which cut and wound people around them. They have

133

no input valve from Me, but feed directly from the sources of the mind arising out of history or from events in the present day. The five senses take in and offer up impressions for the interpretation of the soul. These stony storehouses receive constant shipments of whispered lies from My enemy. These evil substances create a toxic coating upon the heart.

Remember, stone houses do not breathe. There is no life within them. In the darkness and in the lack of refreshment from the truth, heavy mold, slime, and residue build up. This heart will deliver its contents according to its own perceptions and will. It submits to no authority other than to its own desires – all the while making bitter deliveries, unaware that it has given the authority to My enemy to write the invoice, directing the delivery of the heart's unholy contents.

Some of you may not be aware that your heart has become a combination of construction materials and form. You may have a warm rhythmic heart in one chamber, while at the same time, there is a hardened portion being formed in another chamber. Where a thorn of offense or misunderstanding has been lodged in a portion of your heart, an infection of self-defense or self-justification has begun to set up. If this thorn is not pulled, if the lies infecting through your perceptions or memories of the event are not removed and the area cleansed, a hardening effect will begin. If unattended, the stony walls of scar tissue will begin to form until this structure has taken over an entire section of your heart. When this happens, your heart will begin to lose function. It will not be able to receive fully from Me. It will not be able to pour out the love and good things to others without having a mix of the bile arising from the hardened portion. The heart will not come to a place of total refreshment, as its valve to the Spirit becomes partially stuck in a closed position. I cannot bless hypocrisy. You will become weak and ill over time if this condition is not reversed.

In the realities of your physical heart you can see these same processes. There are conditions seen in the human heart where a blockage forms out of plaque over time. Where there has been injury or insult, the plaque attaches to the interior of the blood vessel to become a protective patch. Rather than being healed, the wounds are merely patched. Layers of plaque build up over time. Little by little the vessels of the heart become smaller as the blockage slowly shuts down the flow. If the arteries cannot be cleansed and healed, they will have to be replaced. In some cases of heart conditions, the heart muscle itself loses its ability to pump as a result of a hardening process making the organ rigid. A heart transplant is then the only hope to maintain life. In some cases of heart condition the heart becomes greatly enlarged. It receives the blood, but cannot pass it on. Over time it too loses healthy function or ruptures suddenly bringing on instant death.

Many other parables of the spiritual heart are built within your physical heart. Valves that fail to work properly. Heart muscles that have become too weak to be effective because of years of strain; an assault of bacteria or virus against the heart muscle that takes over the health of the heart making it diseased – these are all signs to you of things that can happen also to your spiritual heart, to your spiritual storehouse of life.

Consider these things, little one. The quality of your life on earth depends upon you understanding these things that are affecting your health. I speak not only of the physical health you require, but more importantly of your spiritual health. As one of My own, you are to be the picture of vibrant health in the spiritual heart. You are to have a rich flow of love and life through you. You are to be a great storehouse, with an immense capacity to pour out to others at My command. Wherever you go, whether into a place overflowing with My presence or one totally deprived of light, you are to be an available supply of My substance to others.

Look to the condition of your heart, little one. What is the structure? What is the building material of your heart? If you have felt heaviness or a bitterness burn in your heart when you see the face of another pass before you, take note of the hardening process already under way. Attend to the changes needed to your heart. If you have felt depleted and weak in loving, check to see if you have been pouring out without being refilled. If you feel love within, but seem to have a ready supply of bitterness appear suddenly upon your lips, tend to the work of rebuilding and cleaning your heart. If you feel cold in your spiritual chest, see this as a sign that you are nearing the end of your ability to love and to prosper.

Come to Me for a total heart transplant. Remember, stone hearts do not breathe, even as stone storehouses do not. My children need hearts that will breathe in the winds of My Spirit to refresh and to nourish them. Remember that stone hearts become moldy and filled with all manner of wickedness. Come to Me, asking Me to break apart the stony structures of your heart. Come to Me for a rebuilding and a healing of your heart. Come to Me for a total transplant if necessary. I am willing and able and ready to do this work.

Know this: in the days ahead, I will pour out My Spirit in a great abundance upon My children. If both the intake valve and the output valve in a pliable, expandable heart are open, a great river of life will pass through you bringing signs and wonders and miracles. Only those who can contain and transmit great quantities of love will be qualified for these blessings. I will not give them to the hearts who are not fully Mine nor fully surrendered as storehouses for whatever I choose to bring and to do. What kind of storehouse are you for Me? What kind would you like to be? Come to Me while there is still time. Allow Me to construct within you all that is necessary; bringing down all that is unholy before Me. Come, so that in the days ahead you will be in delight with Me, while together we bring a flood of life to transform a dying world.

SHARING THE TREASURE

Little one, I have deposited much treasure of love and wisdom within you. This treasure is intended to be offered and freely given to those whom I have determined. It is not yours to freely cast about to those persons you deem ready and worthy to receive it – in a way and a time that you determine to be best.

I call you to love all people, but the way and the manifestation of that love must be directed by Me. Often in your attempt to show unconditional love, your incomplete understanding becomes an enabling force to perpetrate weakness or dependency in someone else. Loving gestures, which are intended to set free, but now misapplied without understanding, can *help* someone to remain locked in a pattern of sin and weakness. Your loving help can become a crutch to a cripple, enabling him to stand, but unable to walk without your support. Not only have you failed to bless the person with true freedom, but in doing this service, you have bound yourself to him, making yourself unavailable to other purposes I have for you. Extend love in the way and in the form I ask of you. Never assume the manifestation of love, which another one of my children needs to receive from you.

There is a time when a soul is open to receive love, and a time when it is unreceptive. Many things can cause the door of receptivity to open or close. I know the nature of these things. At times your love toward someone must remain outside of his awareness. Sometimes it must only surround from a distance rather than embrace full on. A deeply lacerated heart cannot contain the love of another. At times the trust of love has been destroyed by cruelty enacted in the name of love. Often, someone harboring great self-hatred has had his own heart brutally torn apart, so that it cannot contain the love that he sees as undeserved. One whose heart is filled with bitterness has no room to receive love until the bitterness is drained away. I know all these conditions which afflict the heart and many others as well. I want you to know of these things to remind you that I am the great Director as well as the Author of all love.

How are you to share the treasure of love from a surrounding distance? Bless, little one, bless the other person. Envision beauty, joy, peace, and wholeness for the one unreceptive to love's blessings, while praying for these things to become a reality in that life. Conduct acts of kindness for this person in a way that he will not be burdened by them or know who does these things. Lighten his load where I call you to secretly lift it from him. All the while, patiently wait for the door of receptivity to open. Your efforts will not be in vain. Your patient, invisible love will bring forth fruit; for I shall prosper it from the flower of your compassion.

The treasure of My wisdom within you also has its time of sharing and its time of withholding. My way is the way of wisdom as well as the way of love. Life springs from both. However, human pride keeps a lock on the door of the human mind, refusing to allow My wisdom to enter in. If you try to open that locked door by a word of wisdom, you will be frustrated in your efforts. Pride within the locked mind will find its voice against My wisdom abiding within you. It will attack not only the truth but also the one who brings the wisdom in truth. What will open this lock and thereby open the mind's door? Humility and humiliation are two of the tools that can open or break the lock of pride on the mind. Both must be applied by My hand.

Humility comes as I demonstrate the insufficient ability of the mind to understand, to know, and to appropriate truth. The abilities of the mind are so limited in understanding the eternal. The renewed mind of the spirit has been given these abilities, not the mind of the soul. Things of the earth are even a great challenge for the human mind to truly understand. Pride fills in the blanks with theories and assumptions while speaking of them as certain fact. I am the one who will disprove these facts, bringing humility to those in prideful error.

Humiliation is reserved for those who do not respond to My gentle efforts to bring humility to the soul. While humility comes to demonstrate the insufficiency of the human understanding, humiliation comes to show its total failure. Whatever portion of intellectual pride that cannot be removed by humility, I shall address with humiliation to bring it down. Until pride is put down, wisdom cannot be prospered.

Maturity is yet another factor which must be considered when sharing the treasure of wisdom with another. The maturity of which I speak is not necessarily related to the number of years spent upon the earth. The wisdom fed to a child must be of a serving size and quality relative to the ability of the child to consume and digest it. Whether the person is in a childlike state at age sixty or in the state of maturity at age twelve, the wisdom served up to him must be in accordance with his spiritual growth.

I am the only one who can know these true realities of individual maturity. There are many who presume themselves to be aged while being mere babes. There are those who are young in years, but who contain a capacity for receiving great wisdom due to their humility and spiritual maturity. Never look upon someone with your eyes and assume to know what morsels of wisdom they are to receive. Seek only My evaluation and My direction concerning these things. There has been much choking where too much has been given to the immature. There has been much malnourishment where too little has been offered to the qualified.

Little one, open up your treasure house from Me, being generous with the things I have entrusted to you – both your love and your wisdom, sharing freely as I direct you. Never fear that your supply will be depleted. Do not be deterred by considerations of the cost to yourself that may come from being obedient to My call for you to share. As you were created to participate in the work of My heart, you are living in fulfillment to your call as you obey Me to share with others. When you encounter the wounded or prideful, the bitter or the immature – look to Me for your direction. Leave to My hand the breaking of pride and the defense of wisdom. In this way you will remain unencumbered by concerns that are to be Mine. In this way your love and your wisdom will remain pure – perfect treasure that has come from Me to be shared with others by you.

144

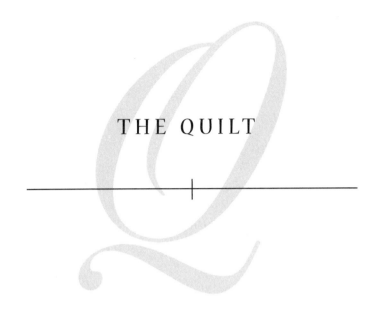

THE QUILT

Be not afraid, little one, of the things that are about to occur in the world, for My hand is over all things. I have cut the pieces of fabric, and have ordered them to create a new quilt out of My faithful ones. From what you now see, you surmise only pieces – unrelated pieces, brokenness, impossible to repair, disorder with little beauty or purpose. Likewise, one without knowledge and without a vision for making a quilt, would also see only a stack of irregular pieces without order before the quilt is assembled. Your assumptions made about the events coming upon the world would lead you to these same conclusions of impossible brokenness. Yet, in these days, know this: I am a skilled Quilt Maker!

I have formed the pieces – not by tearing, but rather by cutting them with My sharp edge of holiness. Things once intact are now cut into pieces. What seemed to be an enduring unity has suddenly become divided. Relationships that lacked true wholeness are now severed. Concealed divided hearts are now clearly seen and separated. Contracts established without truth, but rather founded upon illusions, deceptions, and idolatry have now been broken. Nations established upon unholy compromise or with unholy foundations are now in pieces. Those who have abandoned their once secure and righteous foundations are unable to stand together. The pieces now covering the face of the earth are varied in shape, in size, and in color. More pieces are yet to be cut by My hand. Know this: the same hand that cut these pieces from the fabric gathered throughout the world, will lift up the chosen pieces to reassemble them into something new and glorious.

Await and behold the time of stitching. How is a quilt made, except to stitch one piece to another? One piece to one piece – two become one, three become one, four become one, and so it goes, until the work is complete. While the time of cutting is painful, so also is the process of stitching the pieces together to make a new creation. The stitching requires a sharp instrument, and a piercing penetration of the fabric. It requires a strong thread capable of joining the pieces, to establish and to maintain an enduring bond. The sharp needle I am using in the assembly of My quilt is the reality of the events to come – the trials and the tribulations upon the earth.

The very fabric of My nations and of My people will be penetrated. The institutions and the traditions will be penetrated until the fabric yields to the pull of the thread directed by My hand. The pieces *will* come together. You must not fear. The thread, which shall bring the pieces into oneness, is the substance of My purpose. My fulfilled will is the very thing which shall bring forth a new creation out of all the perceived, mere fragments. Trust me in this.

All the things that seem to be falling chaotically, uncontrollably to pieces, are actually being directed by My hand. I alone hold the shears; the blades of cutting are Mine alone. I decide the shape and the trimming of the fabric. I wield the needle, bringing the sting of its penetration. I also direct the pulling of the thread, even as I am the power to pull it through to its destination.

Do not be discouraged, little one. Do not despair when you see the pieces forming as they fall from My shears. Submit to the blades of the shears as they are applied to your own life. Look past the pain of the needle, and past the pressure of the thread. Look with holy inspired eyes to that which cannot yet be seen in the natural. See with the eyes of the Spirit the masterpiece to come – the masterpiece of the finished quilt. Bless the work of My hand as you yield to it, and as you see it prosper in the world surrounding you. Rest in the truth that My finished quilt shall indeed be glorious.

And you, little one, are to know this: you are a precious piece, cut by the love of My own hand, and shaped with the tenderness of My presence in your life. Find your joy there. Find it in the fact that you are a part of a great, beloved quilt masterpiece that I am making in these days – one that I shall wrap around Myself and which I shall bless with My love throughout all of eternity.

The Call *of the* Shepherd

The sheep

hear the voice

of their Shepherd.

They follow Him,

finding comfort

in His presence.

Seeing truth

in His eyes,

they trust.

In Him

is all truth.

A Concluding Word
to the Reader

It is my prayer that as you have journeyed through these pages, you were able to hear the voice of the Great Shepherd, who dearly loves you. He has called each of us to embrace a deeper walk with Him, and to bear much fruit for His Kingdom. What He has called us to do, He will enable us to accomplish. When we cannot walk, He will carry us. He wants us to trust Him, rather than to be discouraged by our own shortcomings.

The many challenges of our spiritual training are preparing us for a great victory. In the third volume of this trilogy, *The Cry Of The Shepherd*, some tools for securing that victory will be given. The Great Shepherd wants us to know that His ability to bring us through to victory is far greater than the ability of the Enemy to defeat us. Once we truly know His love for us … once we come into a mature relationship with the Shepherd … we will be ready to fight at His side in battle; sharing in His accomplished victory. Now that you have heard His call, listen for His cry resounding over the flock.

In what is yet to come …

"Many will be purged, purified and refined, but the wicked will act wickedly; and none of the wicked will understand, but those who have insight will understand. Daniel 12:10 (NASB)

The Call *of the* Shepherd

THOUGHTS AND REFLECTIONS

To purchase more copies, for information on
distribution, or to view all products available through
DEEPER REVELATION BOOKS

Visit our website:
www.deeperrevelationbooks.org

Phone: 423-478-2843

Mailing address:
P. O. Box 4260
Cleveland, TN 37320